Accession no.
01147431

KU-302-401

Sport,
Leisure Identities
and
Gendered Spaces

2

Edited by

Sheila Scraton and Beccy Watson

1670177
LIBRARY
ACC. No.
0114743 1 | DEPT.
CLASS No.
UNIVERSITY
COLLEGE CHESTER

LSA
Publication No. 67

First published in 2000 by
Leisure Studies Association

The collection as a whole © 2000 LSA
The individual contributions © 2000 the respective authors

All rights reserved. No part of this publication
may be reproduced or transmitted in any form
or by any means without permission
in writing from the LSA.

A catalogue record for this book
is available from the British Library.

ISBN: 0 906337 79 8

Layout design and typesetting by Myrene L. McFee
Printed and bound by Antony Rowe Ltd, Eastbourne

Contents

Editors' Introduction

The articles in this book are drawn from work originally presented at the 4th International LSA Conference, The Big Ghetto: Gender, Sexuality and Leisure held at Leeds Metropolitan University, July 1998. The main theme of the conference provided the opportunity to host concurrently the 2nd International Women and Leisure Conference, the first having been held at the University of Georgia USA in May 1995. The conference title was chosen to encourage the dissemination of the rich diversity of research and scholarly work that has developed in the area over the past few decades. Key aims of the conference were to bring together work from different cultures and countries and to forge links between feminist and pro-feminist work from a range of academic disciplines. The articles in this edited collection represent this rich diversity and the multi-disciplinary nature of the conference. The four other themed and edited volumes also based on work originally presented at LSA 1998 are detailed at the end of this book.

The first three papers in this collection focus on different aspects of gender and the media. **Ian Jones** and **Lesley Lawrence** provide an interesting and original comparison of fans at two very different leisure sites: a soccer ground and a science fiction convention. Their empirical data involving observation, questionnaire and in-depth interviewing illustrates how and why fans construct and maintain their identification with their favourite sports team or media source product. **Lesley Fishwick** and **Kirsty Leach** examine the linguistic construction and reconstruction of gender difference in the television narrative of Wimbledon 1994. Whereas the Jones and Lawrence article focuses on the consumption of different media forms, Fishwick and Leach provide a detailed analysis of sports media production. Their paper demonstrates how women's status as athletes continues to be confined within a dominant masculine discourse. The third paper on the media also draws on a content analysis, whilst including both print and broadcast media. **Caroline Fusco** and **Sandra Kirby** deconstruct the reporting of a sexual abuse case in which a Canadian ice hockey coach is accused of abusing two of his players. Underlying their analysis is a discussion of the homophobia and hetero-sexism often evident in the reporting of such cases. It is only recently that the nature and extent of sexual abuse in sport has received serious attention within academic circles in leisure and sport.

The next five papers in the volume reflect an engagement with the concept of gendered spaces, although in very different contexts. **Gill Clarke**'s paper for example, explores the experiences of a small group of white lesbian Physical Education (PE) students in three higher education institutions in England. She comments that whilst our knowledge of lesbian PE teachers in England and North America has increased, we still have little understanding of the lives of lesbian PE students. Using narratives from their life stories she demonstrates how students cross (hetero)sexual borders and establish 'safe' lesbian havens. The paper by **Jayne Caudwell** also draws on poststructural theories of gender and sexuality in her study of the figure of "the butch" and tomboyism in relation to women who play football in the UK. She argues for a theorisation of gender that allows for an analysis of female masculinity in sport. Whereas Caudwell's article is based upon women's use of a masculine dominated sporting space, **Lynn Embrey** focuses upon softball in Australia from an historical perspective and traces its transformation from a feminine space to one that has become heterosexual. Thus she demonstrates how some men are moving across traditional spatial boundaries within sport, yet without significantly changing dominant gender relations.

Paula Roberts also draws on historical analysis, detailing the life history of Shirley Strickland, one of Australia's most successful Olympic athletes. Roberts argues that her life history depicts a 'gender free' upbringing that encouraged a synthesis of traits previously ascribed to one or the other gender. This she describes as androgynous and regards it as an example of the transformation of gendered space within sport. Strickland succeeded in athletic activities traditionally seen as masculine and overtly competitive in the 1940s and 1950s. In a contemporary context, **Sarah Taylor** and **Scott Fleming** examine women rugby players and the construction of distinctive subcultural identities. They do this by drawing upon the findings of an ethnographic study of a women's rugby club in the UK. The article demonstrates both inclusion and exclusion in gendered spaces and addresses some of the ways in which particular male images, and aspects of masculine identity are adapted by these women rugby players.

The final two papers address the problematic nature of identities, focusing in particular on how different women perceive and experience their bodies in leisure and sport. **Kari Fasting** explores individual recreational women athletes' perceptions of their bodies in a consumer culture. She draws on qualitative data with women participating in aerobics and recreational soccer. She identifies both compliance and resistance to hegemonic femininity within dominant discourse surrounding the 'ideal' female body. The final paper by **Linda Balboul** draws on similar debates, albeit in a very different context. She suggests that many Muslim women in Egypt challenge dominant western idealisations of the female form through their wearing of the veil whilst engaging in various forms of physical activity. This paper provides an insight into cultural and religious debates that still remain at the periphery of leisure and sport studies.

This collection of edited articles from the 4th International Leisure Studies Association Conference draws together papers delivered at the conference around the theme of Sport, Leisure Identities and Gendered Spaces. It reflects the dynamism of feminist research in the broad area of leisure and sport and provides evidence that we are moving out of the 'Big Ghetto'.

Sheila Scraton
Professor of Leisure and Feminist Studies
Centre for Leisure and Sport Research
Leeds Metropolitan University

Dr. Beccy Watson
Senior Lecturer in Leisure and Sport Studies
Centre for Leisure and Sport Research
Leeds Metropolitan University

Identity and Gender in Sport and Media Fandom:
An Exploratory Comparison of Fans attending Football Matches and Star Trek Conventions

Ian Jones and Lesley Lawrence

Department of Tourism and Leisure, University of Luton (UK)

> Fandom is typically associated with cultural forms that the dominant value system denigrates — pop music, romance novels, comics, Hollywood mass-appeal stars (sport, probably because of its appeal to masculinity, is an exception). [Fiske, 1992: p. 30]

Introduction

Fandom is "a common feature of popular culture in industrial societies" (Fiske, 1992: p. 30), and "should be a coherent and important subject for critical inquiry" (Lewis, 1992: p. 2). Yet it is noteworthy that the phenomenon — whether applied to sport or media fandom[1], has received only recent attention from academics, being seen as "trivial" in nature compared to more central aspects of day to day life, such as work, or business (Lewis, 1992; Bromberger, 1993). Although interest in the fan has grown in recent years, such growth has been uneven in the type of questions that have received attention. Certain aspects of fandom, notably those of fan deviance, have received considerable academic observation at the expense of more fundamental issues of fandom. The negative is highlighted rather than the positive.

Where sport is concerned, fans may be "cast as 'couch potatoes' or linked to hooliganism" (Wenner and Gantz, 1998: p. 242). Indeed, it has been noted that most research on sport fans deals with issues of fan violence (Wann and Hamlet, 1995; Burca, *et al.* 1996; Wann, *et al.* 1996). This is a point that has been continually restated. As Duke (1991); Haynes (1995) and Burca, *et al.* (1996) note, there is a fundamental lack of information on the non-hooligan fan as a result of this emphasis. Duke

1

(1991: p. 627) suggests that the major focus of spectator sport in England
— professional football — has been a casualty of this research agenda. He
notes that:

> [a] corollary of this concentration on a form of behaviour involving
> a minority of football spectators has been the neglect of systematic
> empirical research into the majority of the football crowd,

with one outcome being that:

> the Taylor Report on the Hillsborough[2] Stadium Disaster could call
> upon no recent data on the social composition of the football crowd
> in Britain. (Duke, 1991: p. 628)

Not only is the question of who football fans are still largely unanswered
(except for the *Premier League* surveys, which deal only with fans of clubs
at the highest level), but the more interesting question of the meanings of
fandom also remains unresearched. The 1995/96 and 1996/97 *Premier
League* surveys (SNCCFR, 1995; 1996) provide some answers in terms of
measuring social data and behavioural aspects of fans of the more
successful clubs. These surveys, however, have been subject to
methodological criticism (Waddington, *et al.* 1996; Nash, 1997), and have
not been aimed at an academic audience (Williams, 1996). Furthermore,
these surveys do not attempt to investigate significantly beyond overt fan
behaviour such as number of games attended, or money spent on fandom.

Whilst violence features to a much lesser extent, media fandom is not
expressed in the literature as a leisure activity that conforms to the norm.
Jenson (1992: p. 13) contends that very little literature:

> Explores fandom as a normal, everyday cultural or social
> phenomenon. Instead, the fan is characterised as (at least
> potentially) an obsessed loner, suffering from a disease of isolation,
> or a frenzied crowd member, suffering from a disease of contagion.

Similar criticism can be levelled at literature on specific media source
products: for example, fans of daytime soap operas are described as
"abnormal" (Harrington and Bielby, 1995: p. 112), and Star Trek fans are
portrayed as "exotic, unknowable and irrational" (Jenkins and Tulloch,
1995: p. 3). As Jenkins (1991: p. 174) crucially points out:

> behind the exotic stereotypes fostered by the media lies a largely
> unexplored terrain of cultural activity.

Fans of sport, regarded as more 'normal', may be stereotyped as having violent tendencies but tend not to suffer from having their rationality questioned. This difference emerges from literature that does compare media and sports fans. For example, Harrington and Bielby (1995: p. 5), when commenting upon the acceptability or non-acceptability of being a fan by the 'nonfan public', contend that:

> media fans particularly are subject to marginalization because their pleasure derives from fictional narratives rather than from something "real", like a basketball game.

In media fandom, the tendency of fans to "[deny] their own fandom" and carry on "secret lives as fans" (Lewis, 1992: p. 1) is perhaps more likely, though it can be argued that both sport and media fandom suffer in this way — not helped by preconceptions of the many journalists who write negatively about both phenomena. This association of fandom with "immaturity and mindlessness" by critics (McQuail, 1997: p. 36) could arguably be transferred to the world of academia. In relation to media fans, Jenkins (1992: p. 7) views "academic accounts of fan culture as being sensationalistic and foster misunderstandings about this subculture", and Jenkins and Tulloch (1995: p. 5) find academic writers to be "influenced by constructs mapped by popular journalism and preconceived by the reading public". One conclusion, thus, is the need for more research that objectively sets out to reveal 'normal' fan behaviour and attitudes; this would lead in turn to greater understanding of what motivates individuals to be fans, and what it means to be a fan and to belong to a fan community. As Jenkins (1991: p. 197) points out:

> neither the popular stereotype of the crazed Trekkie nor academic notions of commodity fetishism or repetition compulsion are adequate to explain the complexity of fan culture.

With reference to football[3], for example, Tomlinson (1983: p. 9) argues that:

> too much work on football has ... concentrated on the hooliganism aspect, at the expense of our understanding of developments within the culture of the game.

As academics, we would express similar motivations and sentiments to those of Henry Jenkins who, in recalling the aims of his research on media fans, contends that:

> Fans are often represented as antisocial, simple-minded, and
> obsessive. I wanted to show the complexity and diversity of fandom
> as subcultural community. (Jenkins, 1992: p. 277)

This paper attempts to address such imbalance, albeit with a different
focus. We provide a preliminary examination of one element of fandom —
fan identification. In the late 1980s, Wenner and Gantz (1989) recommended future research to compare fan subcultures within different sports.
Our aim, by contrast, is to compare fan identification in two more widely
differing contexts — sport and media. In doing so, we acknowledge the
complexities and differing interpretations of the concept of identification,
which makes the task of finding a unified concept across the contexts of
media and sport highly difficult. Problems of complexity and definition are
ably discussed elsewhere (e.g. Mayne, 1993; Hall, 1996). For our purposes,
the approach taken by Hall (1996: p. 2) is followed, his description of
identification deemed appropriate in both contexts. Hall contends that:

> Identification is constructed on the back of a recognition of some
> common origin or shared characteristics with another person or
> group, or with an ideal, and with the natural closure of solidarity
> and allegiance established on this foundation.

Only a few studies and texts examine how and why fans construct and
maintain an identification with either their favourite sports team or media
source product, in this case, football and Star Trek. Bacon-Smith (1992),
Bromberger *et al.* (1993), Jones (1998), Lewis (1992) and Wann *et al.* (1996)
can be cited as notable exceptions; yet, apart from Jones (1998), none do
so in any substantial way. The study by Jones (1998) was prompted by the
limited research on the actual identities of football fans, especially those at
the lower levels of the Football League. Whilst interest by academics in the
concept of identification is much greater in media studies, theoretical
applications are more varied and crucially tend to be applied to audiences
in general as opposed to fans. In film theory, for example, the
psychoanalytic connection has traditionally been stressed, and linked to
theories of desire; Mayne (1993: p. 22)[4] refers to "the gaze as a primary
structure of identity".

   A gender analysis also underpins our examination of fandom and
identification. Sport is regarded as very much a male domain (Theberge,
1994; Whannel, 1998a). As Whannel (1998a: p. 34) contends:

> sporting practices polarise the genders — most sport is still largely
> dominated by men, whether in terms of participation, spec-
> tatorship, media image, or officialdom.

In referring to different sport contexts, Whannel (1998b: p. 22) suggests that gender may be "a good place to start" when looking at cultural differences. Arguably, the same applies to any comparison across sport and media subcultures. Significantly, media fandom has been referred to as "a vehicle for marginalized subcultural groups (women, the young gays, and so on)" (Jenkins, 1991: p. 174), and as a largely female fan culture (Jenkins, 1992). Star Trek fandom with its prominent female participation has been credited with trend setting: namely, setting "the model for subsequent developments in media fandoms" (Harrison, 1996: p. 259).

The main aim of the data analysis for this paper was to assess the relative identities of the different sets of fans attending football matches and Star Trek conventions (fan-run)[5], and highlighting and explaining any gender differences within and between contexts.

Of a number of characteristics of fandom identified in the literature, one in particular is relevant to our study. Jenkins (1991) suggests, with regard to media fandom, that:

> the ability to transform personal reaction into social interaction, spectatorial culture into participatory culture, is one of the central characteristics of fandom. (Jenkins, 1991: p. 175)

Fans can be viewed as constituting "an elite fraction of the larger audience of passive consumers" (Grossberg, 1992: p. 52). We are interested in this 'elite fraction', in the participant, or in what we are calling the 'active' fan, on whom research is particularly limited. We will therefore begin — or perhaps more aptly kick or beam-off — by raising some issues concerning our interpretation and use of the term 'active fan'. Social identity theory, which provides the main theoretical framework in the paper, is then discussed within the wider consideration of identification, followed by an examination of how gender is treated by academics within the two contexts where fandom is concerned. Our methodology follows; this includes an explanation of the measurement of identity, with particular focus upon the sports fan scale developed by Wann and Branscombe (1993) and its adaptation for use in football and Star Trek contexts. We then discuss the findings from the data collected in the two contexts of football and Star Trek, to arrive at some conclusions.

The active fan: the fan 'engaging with the community'

As previously stated, the comparison here confines itself to one particular category of 'active' fans, namely those who *attend* live football matches or Star Trek conventions. Research is particularly limited with this category of active fan where football and Star Trek fandom is concerned. Attending the convention, for Star Trek fans and many science-fiction fans in general, has been described as providing a means of 'engaging with the community' (Bacon-Smith, 1992), and, as "joining a community of other fans who share common interests" (Jenkins, 1991: p. 175). Arguably one of the more overt ways of engaging with the community, Star Trek conventions normally take place over 2 to 3 days, many with around the clock programmes (late discos and continuous video are the norm for the early morning slots), functioning for the fans as Bacon-Smith describes:

> Conventions spatially and temporally organise the interaction between the community and potential new members, and serve as formal meeting places for the various smaller groups of fans who follow a convention circuit. (Bacon-Smith, 1992: p. 9)

Similarly, football grounds on match day are the main sites for football fans to 'engage with the community'.

Studying one particular form of 'active' fans, namely those who *attend* live football matches or Star Trek conventions, necessitates the exclusion of other individuals, including those who may casually watch an episode or match on the TV and be classed as part of an audience. Those who do attend matches and conventions are also likely to participate in such activities, but the primary criterion for inclusion in our comparative study was attendance at these sites. A parallel could be made with the cinema-goer, with theorists differentiating between watching film on television and film-going as an 'event', necessitating 'going out' (Turner, 1993).

Fans who do not attend matches or conventions may, however, be active in other capacities (for example, collectors of memorabilia, trading cards; contributors to fanzines[6]; involved in artistic enterprises such as costume art; and being fan club members). Lee and Zeiss (1980) give a good example of the maintained consumption of sport away from the actual game event by fans. They characterise a fan as one with a high frequency of indirect consumption, most notably through the media, or by contact with other fans. Similarly, it is suggested that:

> Trekkers do not passively watch television or films but actively use the ideas, symbols and products of mass media and popular culture as personal resources for their own ends as they communicate and interact with one another (Joseph-Witham, 1996: p. 33).

It also needs to be stressed at this point that our usage of the word active should not be confused with the notion of 'the active audience'[7] popularised within Cultural Studies in the 1980s, and used in 'new audience studies' to convey how the audience are "active in their pursuit of pleasure from watching TV — making their own choices and meanings" (Ang, 1996: p. 8). Active in this context places the meaning of the text at the forefront; "the relationship between the audience and popular texts is an active and productive one" (Grossberg, 1992: p. 52). Applied to Star Trek, this meaning of active suggests that fans "actively rework the givens of the *Star Trek* universe to make their own cultural meanings" (Penley, 1991: p. x).

Interest by academics in various types of media audiences, including this form of active audience, is much more visible, and particularly so in cinema and television e.g. Ang, 1985; Pribram, 1988; Corrigan, 1991; Ellis, 1992; Mayne, 1993; Stacey, 1994; and Ang, 1996. Turner (1993: p. 120) talks of the move from psychoanalytic explanations towards a focus on the socially constructed, active female reader of texts — the 'female spectator'. Research on Star Trek fans tends to mirror the situation with media fans as a whole, namely with a bias towards this type of active media fan, often represented by the female writing community (Tulloch and Jenkins, 1995). Thus, in media studies in general, the focus tends to be on the larger entity, namely, on the audience and on spectatorship (as exemplified in article and book titles), rather than on fandom. Even within MediaSport[8] where greater interest on fan cultures might be expected, the focus is not on the fan, and surprisingly, not even on the audience. As Whannel (1998b: p. 227) concludes, "analysis of media sport has tended to focus more on texts and/ or production practices rather than the audience". When audiences have been studied, the focus tends to be on those who watch televised sports (Gantz and Wenner, 1991, 1995), rather than on fans *per se*, or on attendees of live matches. As has been pointed out:

> not everyone who watches sports on television is a fan. The fan is only one part of the television sports spectator picture. (Gantz and Wenner, 1998: p. 234)

This brings us back to the question, what is the difference? Whether attending the game and convention or not, what differentiates a non-fan from a fan? The concept of identification is a major explanatory factor.

Fandom and identification

Both fans and non-fans can enjoy and find pleasure in sport or in a media product, but as Grossberg (1997: p. 222) points out:

> Fandom is different from consumption or simply enjoyment
> (although it may incorporate it) because it involves a certain kind of
> identification or investment.

With regard to sports fans, authors such as Pooley (1978) and Guttman
(1986) suggest that what differentiates a "fan" of a team from a mere
spectator or observer is the level of personal involvement or identification
with the team. As mentioned earlier, this can be manifested in a variety of
ways, and not always at live matches. Fandom can therefore be differentiated from observing, or passive viewing in terms of the development of
an individual's social and personal identity as a fan. It can be argued that
fans attending football matches and Star Trek conventions are generally
likely to be classed as highly identified and additionally, participants in
what Stebbins (1992) labels as 'serious' rather than casual leisure. As
Stebbins (1992: p. 7) argues, of the six qualities associated with being a
participant in serious leisure, the most relevant is the tendency to:

> *identify* strongly with their chosen pursuits ... in contrast,
> unserious leisure, though hardly humiliating or despicable, is
> nonetheless too fleeting, mundane, and commonplace for most
> people to find a distinctive identity within it.

Whilst an individual could be regarded as taking part in serious leisure in
a variety of contexts — for example, the gardener, the solo climber, the
stamp collector — it is the social elements that are often perceived to be at
the heart of fandom. McQuail (1997: p. 36) for example, talks of the:

> potential for media experience to form the basis of distinctive
> subcultures and identifications. Not only are fans often organised
> social groups, but they interact very actively with their object of
> attention and affection.

This emphasis on the 'social' explains why the theory of social identity
(Tajfel, 1982; Tajfel and Turner, 1986) is being regarded as an appropriate
framework for our comparative exploration of fan identification; the entities
that provide fans with the basis for a shared social identity are the products
of specialist fandoms, namely Luton Town football club and Star Trek.

Whilst Pooley (1978: p. 14) implies, rather than explicitly states, that
fandom is strongly related to the individual's personal identity, autonomous
from others, it is usually the social aspect of fandom that is seen as differentiating a fan from a spectator. Thus, from a sporting context it has been
suggested that:

fans perceive themselves as members of a tacitly existing group to which the object of their fanship belongs. (Zillman and Paulus, 1993: p. 604)

And as Jenkins (1991: p. 175) suggests with regard to media fans:

One becomes a 'fan' not by being a regular viewer of a particular program but by translating that viewing into some kind of cultural activity, by sharing feelings and thought about the program content with friends, by joining a 'community' of other fans who share common interests.

Fans can be differentiated from non-fans in terms of the development of an individual's identity as a fan, in that the individual develops three interrelated elements of identification:

- a cognitive element — the individual has an awareness of being a fan;
- an evaluative element — the individual has an awareness of the value of being a fan;
- an emotional element — the individual has an affective involvement of being a fan.

These elements allow the individual to develop both a personal and a social identity as a fan. The personal identity refers to the fan's self-concept ("I am a fan"). The social identity refers to the relationships that are formed as a fan ("I am a fan of club 'X' or media source product"). Both forms of identity are interrelated, in that a social identity, or feeling of group membership, will influence the individual's sense of who they are, or their personal identity. The individual's desired personal identity, that is their sense of who they want to be, will influence the social identities that they attempt to create. The overall goal is to maintain a positive personal and social identity (Tajfel, 1982; Brown, 1986).

Although not explicitly researched, the awareness of being identified and cognitive and affective involvement with the team or with the media product, as well as the behavioural consequences of such identification, have been discussed by a number of authors.

First, awareness of how the group are identified by outsiders rather than by the group themselves has certainly featured where Star Trek fandom is concerned. Tulloch and Jenkins talk about how fans actively resist portrayal as a 'trekkie', this being:

an identity imposed upon the group from the outside. 'Trekker' came to refer to the group's self-constructed and more affirmative identity. (Tulloch and Jenkins, 1995: p. 15)

Second, Branscombe and Wann (1992: p. 1017) incorporate cognitive and affective reactions to events when they define sports fan identification, referring to the concept as:

the extent to which individuals perceive themselves as fans of the team, are involved with the team, are concerned with the team's performance, and view the team as a representation of themselves.

The importance of the affective experience as contributing to the media fan's identity is particularly stressed by Grossberg (1992) and Harrington and Bielby (1995).

As well as the perception that the individual will have of being a fan, there are behavioural consequences of identification, and individuals may well display other characteristics of group membership. Generally where group membership is concerned, these have been identified variously as:

• ethnocentrism, or seeing the group to which the fan belongs (i.e. other football fans, for example) as "special" (Oakes and Turner, 1980; Hogg and Vaughn, 1995);

• strong cohesiveness, or willingness to remain in the group (Cartwright, 1953; Baron and Byrne, 1994);

• conflict with, or derogation of other groups (Tajfel, 1982; Branscombe and Wann, 1992; Wann and Dolan, 1994), especially those seen as rivals (Sherif, 1966); and

• strong indirect contact with the focus of identity, through personal, or indirect contact (McPherson, 1975; Pooley, 1978; Smith, et al. 1981).

Fans may also be able to enhance self esteem as a consequence of their identification, through the process of "basking in reflected glory", or "BIRGing" (Cialdini, et al. 1976; Madrigal, 1995).

It is possible to apply most of the above to Star Trek fandom, but the areas of conflict and rivalry cause differences to emerge. Whilst in football fandom the 'winning of the game' is highly influential in creating loyalty, rivalry and conflict, Star Trek fandom has less easily defined boundaries between groups, weaker identity with one group or media product, and arguably less rivalry. Not only within Star Trek fandom are there a number of different communities where divisions and rivalries might emerge, but unlike football, where often the loyalty and identity rests with one particular team, in media fandom, identification is not always just with one product. Bacon-Smith (1992) gives a fairly succinct explanation of identity and priorities in media fandom. She suggests fans usually have a primary identity where one genre is the favourite and within this one medium or delivery channel with a particular attraction within this to a particular product (e.g. Star Trek or Babylon 5) and an activity (e.g. attending conventions, contributing to fanzines). At the same time, complicating the situation somewhat, "media fans can take pleasure in making intertextual connections across a broad range of media texts" (Jenkins, 1992: p. 36), and they may "drift from one series commitment to another" (Jenkins, 1992: p. 41).

Gender in sport and media fandom

As stated earlier, gender analysis also underpins our examination of fandom and identification; the authors perceived the likelihood of gender issues emerging as one advantage of choosing to compare football and Star Trek fandom. This was based upon several factors, the first being specific to sport and media as a whole rather than to fandom in the two contexts, namely, the believed predominance of male cultural hegemony in both sport (e.g. Rowe, 1995; Wearing, 1998) and media (e.g. Wearing, 1998). The other factors relate to how gender tends to be treated by academics in both sport and media fandom:

- the amount of gender-driven research and gender-informed comment-ary is based largely upon the male in sport and football fandom, and by contrast upon the female in media and Star Trek fandom;
- the relatively little gender comparison within contexts is notable;
- a notable amount of academic literature in media fandom is gender driven and largely feminist-based; a gender emphasis is lacking where sport and football fandom are concerned.

Gantz and Wenner (1995: p. 60) note the paucity of writing on the "issue of gender and fanship" in the sports context; additionally, gender comparison research in sport fandom and more specifically, football fandom is not readily available. Existing works tend to either investigate the male sports fan in isolation (e.g. Smith, *et al.* 1981; King, 1997), or treat sports fans as an homogenous mass, without reference to gender (such as Madrigal 1995; Wann, *et al.* 1996).

A largely male fan culture exists at football matches (SNCCFR, 1995, 1996), not only characterised by masculinity, but also by particular types of masculinity, such as the highly committed male fan (Smith, *et al.*, 1981), the violent male fan (Dunning, *et al.* 1986) or the "Lads" (King, 1997). Given the dominance of research on the hooligan, the dearth of research on female fans or even on issues, is perhaps unsurprising. Literature on the football hooligan, as opposed to the fan, focuses almost exclusively on the male, for example, upon the centrality of the expression of a particular masculine identity, or what refers to as a "violent masculine style", displayed by working class, hard core hooligans (Dunning, 1994: p. 174). As Haynes (1993: p. 57) points out, studies on football hooliganism attempt to "analyse football and masculinity, albeit in the context of violence".

Woodhouse (1990) and Williams and Woodhouse (1991) have provided preliminary examinations of female football fans, however little empirical evidence is available upon the female football fan, other than the Premier League surveys (SNCCFR 1995, 1996), which provide mostly descriptive information upon such fans' patterns of behaviour. Going somewhat against the norm, Haynes (1993) examines the role played by the media in analysing the reproduction of masculinity in football, not confining his discussion to theories of football and masculinity, but also discussing feminist cultural theory and football. Perhaps Brown's summary paints the more realistic picture? He points out that:

> although there have been key developments around the issue of gender in football — increasing numbers of females attending games in the UK, participation of women in Italian *ultrá* groups, the increased marketing of the game to young women — this is not reflected in academic literature and research. (Brown, 1998: p. 7)

Rather ironically, Brown (1998: p. 7) acknowledges this omission in the text he was editing which was seeking "to consider processes of exclusion and participation in football"; he gives a rather half-hearted plea for research on the issue of gender. Such omissions do nothing to rectify impressions voiced by Chorbajian (1978: p. 165), who suggested that:

> not only do more men watch than women; they generally watch with greater interest, sophistication, and emotional involvement.

The outlook is much healthier where television sports viewing is concerned with gender analysis more prominent (e.g. by Davis, 1990; Messner and Sabo, 1990; Gantz and Wenner, 1995; Wenner and Gantz, 1998). The realisation that the sports audience is not just one homogeneous mass has dawned, and as Wenner (1998: p. 11) points out, the potential of audience research, "in particular, research on how fanship and gender interact with audience experience holds real promise".

Where Star Trek is concerned, a similar picture can be painted of limited gender comparison, and of a gender bias, though this time directed towards the study of female fans and audiences. Relatively recently, Brunsdon (1997: p. 35) talks of the prominence of feminist research in more recent media research studies and the "growing literature on audiences-as-fans and fan identity as such", citing examples from Star Trek , and from music videos, thus giving a certain degree of credence and highlight to the study of Star Trek within Media Studies. Critics and fans have credited Star Trek with bringing the first mass female audience to the science fiction genre (Harrison *et al.*, 1996) and Star Trek fandom has been "the model for subsequent developments in media fandoms" (Harrison, 1996: p. 259). According to Harrington and Bielby, (1995: p. 5), Star Trek is regarded as the "most widely studied subculture of media fans" and this is predominantly from a feminist perspective (e.g. Bacon-Smith, 1992; Helford, 1996; Projansky, 1996; Penley, 1997). One of the more prominent studies of Star Trek fandom is Bacon-Smith's ethnography based on the sub-community of fans [predominantly women] who create and distribute fiction and art (the text was entitled 'Enterprising Women — Television Fandom and the Creation of Popular Myth'. Many female fans create derivative narratives "partly as a way of claiming space in male-centred texts" (Jenkins, 1988: p. 89); and it is this that attracts feminist analyses of fans. "The meaning of gender — specifically, the position of women in the future — is a dominant discourse interwoven in and guiding Trek's play" (Bernardi, 1998: p. 115).

Feminist research on fans can be found in a range of other television products, for example, *Dallas* (Ang, 1985); *Cagney and Lacey* (Clark, 1990); *Dynasty* (Press, 1990); *Thirtysomething* (Heide, 1995); *Inspector Morse* (Thomas, 1997); *L.A. Law* (Mayne, 1997). Where soap opera is concerned, Livingstone (1994: p. 444) makes the point that "not only are soap opera fans typically women ... the non-fans and media critics are more often men". It was feminist work that began to take soap opera fans seriously (Brunsdon, 1997: p. 42) and, is arguably also responsible for beginning to redress the imbalance. Such interest is found in most media forms:

> Feminists have long recognised the significance of the media as a site for the expression of — or challenges to — existing gender relations. (Van Zoonen, 1994, back cover)

Audiences are usually at the "core of their projects" (Van Zoonen, 1994: p. 103) with the term 'feminine discourse' adopted by academic feminists when discussing how women are addressed in television programmes or films (Brown, 1994). Yet, disquiet is often expressed over the inadequacy of audience research, for instance, in Film Studies. Stacey (1994: p. 12), for example, talks of the reluctance on the part of feminist film theorists to venture into the area of audience research, whilst "all too frequently, women's participation in the 'cinematic experience' has been neglected or entirely overlooked" (Pribham, 1988: p. 1), reflecting the lack of interest in contemporary movie audiences in film studies (Gripsrud, 1998). Whilst Mayne (1993: p. 43) considers that the "female spectator was largely excluded by the 1970s film theory", in 1975 what is widely acknowledged as a pivotal feminist inquiry into the nature of the audience or spectator in film, was published. Mulvey's (1975) 'Visual Pleasure and Narrative Cinema', showed the spectator as being firmly constructed as masculine.

Significantly within Media Studies, much less attention is paid to "the problems arising — in texts and for audiences — from the secure and comfortable 'norm' of masculinity" (Cohan and Hark, 1993: p. 2), or to men and the male image (Neale, 1993). Where the development of audience ethnography is concerned, for example, Moore (1993) mentions the key omission of masculine reading pleasures and competencies; he believes that existing work lacks "the rich insights offered by feminist work" (p. 49). And when masculinity is analysed, it is often from a feminist perspective; for example, Helford (1996) focuses upon masculinity in Star Trek, but does so through feminist textual analysis.

Methodology: the measurement of football and Star Trek fan identification

The chosen instrument to measure fan identification was the *Sport Spectator Identification Scale*, a measure shown both to be valid and reliable (Wann and Branscombe, 1993). This instrument consists of a seven item scale, allowing the strength of identification to be ascertained (**Figure 1**). This scale was initially included within a questionnaire administered to football fans at Luton Town Football Club[9] in 1997. A random stratified sample was employed, whereby every third entrant to the match was handed a questionnaire packet containing the questionnaire, a covering letter, and a pre-paid reply envelope. Twelve-hundred questionnaires were distributed with five hundred and thirty-one being returned — a response rate of 44.3%.

Several issues can be raised over the usage of such a measure. First, the measurement of identification assumes that individuals will have identities that are stable enough to be measured (cf. Widdecombe and Wooffitt (1995: p. 109). Although Turner (1982) notes that identities may vary with the immediate context and environment within which the identity is enacted, work on general social identity theory (Tajfel and Turner, 1986) and sports fan identification theory (Murrell and Dietz, 1992) suggests that

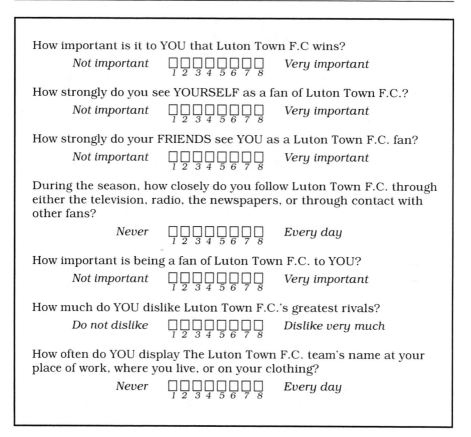

How important is it to YOU that Luton Town F.C wins?

   Not important   ☐☐☐☐☐☐☐☐   *Very important*
               1 2 3 4 5 6 7 8

How strongly do you see YOURSELF as a fan of Luton Town F.C.?

   Not important   ☐☐☐☐☐☐☐☐   *Very important*
               1 2 3 4 5 6 7 8

How strongly do your FRIENDS see YOU as a Luton Town F.C. fan?

   Not important   ☐☐☐☐☐☐☐☐   *Very important*
               1 2 3 4 5 6 7 8

During the season, how closely do you follow Luton Town F.C. through either the television, radio, the newspapers, or through contact with other fans?

        Never   ☐☐☐☐☐☐☐☐   *Every day*
               1 2 3 4 5 6 7 8

How important is being a fan of Luton Town F.C. to YOU?

   Not important   ☐☐☐☐☐☐☐☐   *Very important*
               1 2 3 4 5 6 7 8

How much do YOU dislike Luton Town F.C.'s greatest rivals?

   Do not dislike   ☐☐☐☐☐☐☐☐   *Dislike very much*
               1 2 3 4 5 6 7 8

How often do YOU display The Luton Town F.C. team's name at your place of work, where you live, or on your clothing?

        Never   ☐☐☐☐☐☐☐☐   *Every day*
               1 2 3 4 5 6 7 8

Figure 1   **The football fan identification scale**

identities should remain stable. Empirical support can also be found elsewhere (Branscombe and Wann, 1991; Wann and Branscombe, 1993), arguing that identification remains reasonably constant, even despite team failure or success (Wann and Schrader, 1996). In addition, no differences have been found between those who completed the test either pre-game or post-game (Wann and Dolan, 1994).

A second issue is whether the measure can be adapted for usage in another context. To enable a comparison to be made between football and Star Trek fan identification, the *sport spectator identification scale* had to be adapted for Star Trek fans. Of the seven items, five were readily adaptable. Two items, however, raise potential issues. Firstly, the Star Trek equivalent of 'winning' was not easily definable. Given the self-esteem benefits of success in sports fandom, it was felt that 'a favourable reception to the series' would allow the same mechanisms of "basking in reflected glory" (Cialdini, *et al.* 1976) as winning would for a football team. Secondly, the dislike of rivals, although not problematic to adapt, could be anticipated to result in differences between the two contexts. Sherif (1966) suggests that those group members, i.e. fans of teams with mutually exclusive goals (for example football teams) would show greater dislike of rivals than those with non mutually exclusive goals, for example fans of Star Trek. Thus, it could be predicted that the football fan responses for this item would be higher than the Star Trek fans. The adapted scale is shown in **Figure 2**.

The Star Trek identification scale was included as part of a semi-structured interview conducted with fans at the Scottish Star Trek held at Glasgow in 1998, aimed at exploring several aspects of Star Trek fandom. Over the course of the 3 day convention, 30 attendees were interviewed, with a quota random sample employed to ensure equal numbers of females and males). Interviews ranged from 30 minutes to 1 hour 30 minutes.

How important is it to YOU that Star Trek gets favourably received by other people, e.g. press, media, friends, others?

    Not important ☐☐☐☐☐☐☐☐ *Very important*
                 1 2 3 4 5 6 7 8

How strongly do you see YOURSELF as a fan of Star Trek?

    Not at all a fan ☐☐☐☐☐☐☐☐ *Very much a fan*
                 1 2 3 4 5 6 7 8

How strongly do your FRIENDS see YOU as a fan of Star Trek?

    Not at all a fan ☐☐☐☐☐☐☐☐ *Very much a fan*
                 1 2 3 4 5 6 7 8

During this year, how closely have you kept abreast of happenings in the universe of Star Trek, e.g. through either television, magazines, or through contact with other fans?

    Never ☐☐☐☐☐☐☐☐ *Every day*
                 1 2 3 4 5 6 7 8

How important is being a fan of Star Trek to YOU?

    Not important ☐☐☐☐☐☐☐☐ *Very important*
                 1 2 3 4 5 6 7 8

How much do YOU dislike Star Trek's greatest rivals?

    Do not dislike ☐☐☐☐☐☐☐☐ *Dislike very much*
                 1 2 3 4 5 6 7 8

How often do YOU display The Star Trek's logo/name at your place of work, where you live, or on your clothing?

    Never ☐☐☐☐☐☐☐☐ *Always*
                 1 2 3 4 5 6 7 8

Figure 2   **The Star Trek fan identification scale**

In terms of internal validity, or the extent to which each of the subscales was measuring the same construct, that of fan identification with Luton Town, an acceptable Cronbach alpha score of 0.73 emerged. Fan identification at the Star Trek conference scored 0.82. De Vaus (1985) suggests that any score above 0.70 should be considered as reliable. The differences in nature and scale of the data collection in the two contexts, coupled with tampering with the original validated measure, nevertheless suggests caution when comparisons are being made between contexts (hence, the absence of statistical testing). This all signifies that this overall comparative research be classed merely as a preliminary examination.

The football and Star Trek sample characteristics

The characteristics of each sample are shown in **Table 1**.

Table 1   Sample Characteristics

	Star Trek fans
• n=514	• n=30
• 88.2% male, 11.8% female	• 50% male, 50% female
• mean age 37.8 (male 38.2, female 34.7)	• mean age 29.0 (male 27.6, female 30.4)
• attended for a mean of 21.9 years (male 22.7, female 16.0)	• attended for a mean of 5.5 years (male 5.7, female 5.3)
• went to first match with father (47.9%) or friends (20.2%) rather than alone (4.2%)	• went to first conference alone (33.3%) with friends (33.4%), or with other relatives (23.35) rather than with parents (6.7%)
• attend mainly with family (40.0%) or friends (34.8%) rather than alone (10.2%)	• attend mainly with other relatives (30%) friends (23.3%), or alone (16.7%) rather than with parents (6.7%)
• most (81.7%) support only one team	• No clear identification with one particular Star Trek series[10].

Findings and discussion

Identification: contexts

As shown in **Table 2**, the overall identity mean scores for football and Star Trek were 6.68 and 5.54 respectively (scores range from a minimum 1 to a maximum identification score of 8). Fans of both contexts were thus highly identified with the focus of their fandom. Whilst this is entirely predictable in that the sample were actively 'engaging with the community' through attendance at either a football match or Star Trek convention, a number of other points of interest have been identified.

Table 2   Identification Scale: context differences

	Scale Item	Context	(mean scores)
1	How strongly do you see yourself as a fan of 'X'?	Football	7.50
		Star Trek	7.63
2	How strongly do your friends see you as a fan of 'X'?	Football	**7.37**
		Star Trek	6.80
3	How closely do you follow 'X' through the media, or through contact with other fans?	Football	**7.29**
		Star Trek	5.63
4	How important is being a fan of 'X' to you?	Football	**7.33**
		Star Trek	5.38
5	How often do you display the logo of 'X' at home, at the place where you work, or on your clothing?	Football	5.38
		Star Trek	5.70
6	How much do you dislike 'X's greatest rivals?	Football	**4.86**
		Star Trek	2.97
7	How important is it that 'X' wins/is favourably received?	Football	**7.00**
		Star Trek	3.27
	Overall identity score	Football	**6.68**
		Star Trek	5.54

Bold *indicates a difference of greater than 0.50 in the mean score*

A number of differences emerged between football and Star Trek fan identification. That football fans were more highly identified seem to be as a consequence of a number of differences in the identification scale items. Although Star Trek fans' personal identities, that is how strongly they saw themselves as fans (item 1), were slightly higher than football fans, their social identities, that is how they perceived others to see them as fans (item 2), were lower. The latter could be explained by the likelihood of Star Trek fans denying "their own fandom" and carrying on "secret lives as fans" as has been previously suggested (Lewis, 1992: p. 1). Fan contact (item 3) was also lower for Star Trek fans, although this is predictable given the greater amount of media coverage devoted to football compared to Star Trek.

The mean score for the importance of being a fan (item 4) was lower for Star Trek fans. This may be attributable to the single focus of identification for football fans, who tended to support a single team. As was shown in Table 1, Star Trek fans by contrast tended to identify with more than one single form of Star Trek, which finds support in the literature (e.g. Bacon-Smith, 1992; Jenkins, 1992).

When comparing means scores found for 'dislike of rivals' and 'success' (items 6 and 7), the difference in the mean scores may be attributable to the nature of the context. Star Trek fans were discovered to have no clear identification with a single series, and thus were likely to identify with other products within the same genre. Indeed, 10% of the Star Trek convention attendees revealed that Babylon 5 was the series with which they most identified, in preference to a version of Star Trek. And, those attendees who identified most with Star Trek (77%), were split between different series. Thus, success in this context is not mutually exclusive, in that it is possible for all forms to be equally successful. Most football fans by contrast identified with a single team, in a context where success is mutually exclusive. The findings in this respect support Sherif (1966) who suggests that conflict between groups is likely to be higher for goals that are mutually exclusive. Thus football fans showed dislike of their rivals, and a desire to be successful to a greater extent than did their Star Trek counterparts. Interestingly, 60% of the Star Trek convention attendees when asked whether they believed rivalry existed within Star Trek fandom, responded in the affirmative, with the main source being Star Trek v. Babylon 5, or between the Star Trek series.

Identification: gender

As shown in **Table 3** (page following), when the overall identity scores are broken down by gender, all categories of fans (male football, female football,

Table 3   Identification Scale: gender differences

	Scale Item	Gender Difference — Football (mean scores)		Gender Difference — Star Trek (mean scores)		Context Differences Fb: football ST: Star Trek	
1	How strongly do you see yourself as a fan of 'X'?	M	7.50	M	7.33	Fb	7.50
		F	7.53	F	7.93	ST	7.63
2	How strongly do your friends see you as a fan of 'X'?	M	7.37	M	6.80	Fb	7.37
		F	7.35	F	6.80	ST	6.80
3	How closely do you follow 'X' through the media, or through contact with other fans?	M	7.30	M	5.33	Fb	7.29
		F	7.27	F	5.93	ST	5.63
4	How important is being a fan of 'X' to you?	M	7.32	M	5.29	Fb	7.33
		F	7.37	F	6.03	ST	5.38
5	How often do you display the logo of 'X' at home, at the place where you work, or on your clothing?	M	5.29	M	5.13	Fb	5.38
		F	6.03	F	6.27	ST	5.70
6	How much do you dislike 'X's greatest rivals?	M	4.87	M	2.87	Fb	4.86
		F	4.77	F	3.07	ST	2.97
7	How important is it that 'X' wins/is favourably received?	M	7.00	M	3.27	Fb	7.00
		F	7.03	F	3.27	ST	3.27
	Overall identity score	M	6.67	M	5.27	Fb	6.68
		F	6.76	F	5.81	ST	5.54

male Star Trek, female Star Trek) show relatively high identity scores, ranging from 5.27 for male Star Trek fans to 6.76 for female football fans.

The stereotypical view of football as a male oriented sport is supported only in terms of numbers of male fans, and not in terms of their levels of identification, with female fans showing slightly higher identification mean scores. Only a small (0.09) difference emerged between male and female football fans in contrast to the larger (0.54) difference found between male and female Star Trek fans. In terms of football fan identification, few gender differences emerged in the scale items, with the only difference larger than 0.5 being that female football fans were more likely to display the teams logo than male fans (item 5). In certain respects such findings are surprising in that it might have been expected that differences would be found between male and female fans. Evidence to support the findings and to challenge this assumption, however, comes from comparisons of gender composition within and between groups of television-watching fans and non-fans. Research on television audiences of sport undertaken by Wenner and Gantz (1998: p. 245), for example, shows that "male and female fans are more likely to differ from both male and female non-fans than they are from each other".

It is noteworthy that females were more highly identified in both contexts. Females showed scores higher by 0.50 in four of the seven scale items, and also for the overall identification score. Of the other scale items, substantial differences did not emerge in either the dislike of rivals (item 6) or the importance of success (item 7), which, as indicated above, gave relatively low scores. The other item with no difference was that of social identity, or how strong friends saw the individual as a fan (item 2). Thus, there is some evidence here to suggest that females have stronger fan identities in the Star Trek context.

Concluding comments

Within our broader exploration of gender and identity in sport and media fandom, this paper has provided a preliminary examination of one element of fandom — fan identification. Several conclusions can be reached, not only with regard to the findings themselves, but pertaining to the perceived usefulness of this form of study and the emergence of research implications.

Twenty years ago, Anderson noted that the sports fan had been "virtually ignored by most researchers" (1979: p. 116). Arguably, the same accusation could be levelled at the academic community today regarding the noted lack of interest in a number of related issues within sport and media fandom. This applies in particular, to the process and role of identification. Our findings suggest that identity is inexorably linked to, and plays a key role, not only in understanding fandom in both football and Star Trek, but within sport and media fandom as a whole; yet, its study appears limited. Equally, gender comparison within contexts is also notable by its relative absence. Whilst gender comparisons are beginning to be reported with television audiences and fans (e.g. Wenner and Gantz, 1998), what about our 'active' fan and other fan activities?

In one sense, it could be argued that the lack of research on fandom is unsurprising given the connotations of triviality and non-seriousness often associated with the study of fans. The academic community does not generally regard fan activity as a leisure norm, though such activity may be perceived as a main leisure activity for fans themselves. Given the size of the 'normal' fan bases in both contexts, and the seriousness with which many such fans take their fandom, the potential for research by leisure scholars seems untapped and the need for study, paramount. For example, specific areas of potential study may be on the causes or antecedents of fan identification or the influence of fan identification on behaviour as just two examples.

In terms of the use of a comparative study, rather than investigating the sports fan, or the media fan alone, the approach is useful – indeed, Durkheim (1938: p. 125) suggests that such an approach is "the only one suited to sociology". Given the lack of existing empirical research, gender was considered as a suitable focus upon which to base the comparison, given Whannel's (1998b: p. 22) argument outlined earlier within the paper that gender is "a good place to start" when looking at cultural differences in the sports context. Whilst agreeing with Whannel's sentiments, we would argue that gender also forms a useful focus when comparing across, as well as within popular cultures.

The comparative method has also indicated the need for future research into gender and fan identification, with reference to specific forms of fandom, given that gender differences did emerge – to some extent – in one form, but not the other. The comparative method allows such differences in cultures to be identified. Why is it, for example, the case that females were as highly identified as males in a traditionally male context (at a football match), yet male fans were not as highly identified in the stereotypically female environment of the Star trek convention? In issues such as these, the comparative method is useful in developing such questions.

In terms of our comparison, our analysis using an adapted identification scale to measure identification can itself be accused of being rather limited; for example, surely qualitative data would give greater insight? We are aware of the limitations of using such a scale, however, and also of the need for such qualitative insight; the data analysed for the purposes of this paper did, in fact, come from wider databases in both con-texts — interview and participant observation data were not utilised. Thus, there is scope to add to this preliminary comparison from the authors' own data and also to further explore and test some of the findings identified in this paper. This would enable less speculative explanations of, for example: the greater identification scores of football fans compared to Star Trek fans;

the greater identification scores of female Star Trek fans when compared to their male counterparts; and why no notable differences emerged between genders in the football context.

The lack of attention to qualitative data has also led to no discussion of interesting issues that emerged in our research, pertaining to researcher roles and dilemmas when studying fan cultures as academics and as fans, linked to gender nuances within the two contexts.

Notes

[1] Whilst the exact composition of media fandom varies and is subject to much debate, for the purposes of this paper, media fandom is being described as 'relating to live action movies and television' (Bacon-Smith, 1992: p. 7). We would include soap opera in media fandom, though this is not always the case. Similarities can be found between Star Trek and soap opera fandom, in particular in how fans of each often rework the programme to produce their own narratives and texts. Sport fandom is easier to define, and relates to the support of a particular team or player, in the context of this paper watching the sport "live".

[2] The Hillsborough disaster refers to the events of April 15 1989, when "operational errors" led to part of the ground becoming fatally overcrowded, leading to the deaths of ninety-six football fans, mainly as a result of crushing or asphyxiation within a fenced enclosure (Taylor 1990, Williams 1994).

[3] By football, we are referring to the soccer version and not American football.

[4] Whilst space precludes discussion here, Mayne (1993) provides a useful account of the various ways that film theorists have conceived of 'identification in the cinema' through history, its redefinition, the assumptions made, and the problematic nature of the concept.

[5] Star Trek conventions have been classified as either professionally-run (commercial) or fan-run (charity). Our interest is in the latter. Within the fan community, feelings can be quite high over the supposed exploitation of fans where the former is concerned.

[6] Fanzines "are publications devoted to discussing the intricacies and nuances of a cultural genre" (Duncombe, 1997: p. 9), with identifiable subcategories such as football zines, Star Trek zines.

[7] Nightingale (1997) gives an useful insight into the development of the notion of the 'active audience' using several television programmes to illustrate the concept.

8 MediaSport — Wenner (1998) talks of recent moves in academia — "the cultural fusing of sport with communication has resulted in a new genetic strain called *MediaSport*" emerging largely from "two quarters, media studies, in the discipline of communication, and sport sociology" (p. 6).

9 Luton Town Football Club plays in Division 2 in England.

10 Four different series of Star Trek have been created, in chronological order: The Original Series (Classic Trek), The Next Generation; Deep Space Nine; and Voyager.

References

Anderson, D. (1979) 'Sport spectatorship; an appropriation of identity or appraisal of self?', *Review of Sport and Leisure*, Vol. 4, No. 2: pp. 115–127.

Ang, I. (1985) *Watching Dallas: Soap opera and the melodramatic imagination*. London: Methuen.

———— (1996) *Living room wars — rethinking media audiences for a postmodern world*. London: Routledge.

Bacon-Smith, C. (1992) *Enterprising women — television fandom and the creation of popular myth*. Philadelphia: University of Pennsylvania Press.

Baron, R. and Byrne, D. (1994) *Social psychology: Understanding human interaction*. Boston: Allyn and Bacon.

Bernardi, D. L. (1998) *Star Trek and history — racing toward a white future*. New Brunswick: Rutgers University Press.

Branscombe, N. and Wann, D. (1991) 'The positive social and self-concept consequences of sports team identification', *Journal of Sport and Social Issues* Vol. 15, No. 1: pp. 115–127.

———— (1992) 'The role of identification with a group on arousal, categorisation processes and self-esteem in the Sports Spectator, *Human Relations* Vol. 45, No. 10: pp. 1013–1033.

Bromberger, C. (1993) 'Fireworks and the ass', in Redhead, S. (ed) *The passion and the fashion: Football fandom in the new Europe* Aldershot: Avebury Press, pp. 89–102.

Brown, A. (1998) 'Introduction', in A. Brown (ed) *Fanatics! Power, identity and fandom in football*. London: Routledge, pp. 1–7.

Brown, M.E. (1994) *Soap opera and women's talk — the pleasure of resistance*. Thousand Oaks: Sage.

Brown, R. (1986) *Social psychology* (2nd edition). New York: Free Press.

Brunsdon, C. (1997) *Screen tastes — soap opera to satellite dishes*. London: Routledge.

Burca, S. Brannick, T. and Meenaghan, T. (1996) 'Spectators as consumers: A relationship marketing approach, in *Conference Proceedings from the Fourth European Congress on Sport Management*. Montpellier, 2–5 October 1996, pp. 106–118.

Cartwright, D. (1953) 'The nature of group cohesiveness', in D. Cartwright and A. Zander (eds) *Group dynamics: Research and theory*. London: Tavistock Press, pp. 245–265.

Chorbajian, L. (1978) 'The social psychology of American males and spectator sports', *International Journal of Sport Psychology*, Vol. 9: pp. 165–175.

Cialdini, R. Borden, R. Thorne, A. Walker, M. Freeman, S. and Sloan, L. (1976) 'Basking in reflected glory; three (football) field studies', *Journal of Personality and Social Psychology* Vol. 34, No. 3: pp. 366–375.

Clark, D. (1990) 'Cagney and Lacey: Feminist strategies of detection', in M. Brown (ed) *Television and women's culture — the politics of the popular*. London: Sage, pp. 117–133.

Cohan, S. and Hark, I.R. (1993) 'Introduction', in S. Cohan and I. R. Hark (eds) *Screening the male — exploring masculinities in Hollywood cinema*. London: Routledge, pp. 1–8.

Corrigan, T. (1991) *A cinema without walls — movies and culture after Vietnam*. London: Routledge.

de Vaus, D. (1985) *Surveys in social research*. London: UCL Press.

Davis, L.R. (1990) 'Male cheerleaders and the naturalization of gender', in M. Messner (ed) *Sport, men and the gender order — critical feminist perspectives*. Champaign: Human Kinetics, pp. 158–161.

Duke, V. (1991) 'The sociology of football: a research agenda for the 1990s', *Sociological Review*, Vol. 39, No. 3: pp. 627–645.

Duncombe, S. (1997) *Notes from underground — zines and the politics of alternative Culture*. London: Verso.

Dunning, E. (1994) 'Sport as a male preserve: Notes on the social sources of masculine identity and its transformations', in S. Birrell and C. Cole (eds) *Women, sport, and culture*. Champaign: Human Kinetics, pp. 163–179.

Dunning, E., Murphy, P., and Williams, J. (1986) 'Spectator violence at football matches: Towards a sociological explanation', in N. Elias and E. Dunning (eds) *Quest for excitement: Sport and leisure in the civilising process*. Oxford: Basil Blackwell. pp. 245–266.

Durkheim, E. (1938) *The rules of sociological method*. Chicago: Free Press.

Ellis, J. (1992) *Visible fictions — cinema: Television, video* (Revised edition). London: Routledge.

Fiske, J. (1992) 'The cultural economy of fandom', in L. Lewis (ed) *The adoring audience — fan culture and popular media*. London: Routledge, pp. 30–49.

Gantz, W. and Wenner, L.A. (1991) 'Men, women and sports: audience experiences and effects', *Journal of Broadcasting and Electronic Media*, Vol. 35, No. 2: pp 233–243.

—— (1995) 'Fanship and the television sports viewing experience' *Sociology of Sport Journal*, Vol. 12, No. 1: pp 56–74.

Gripsrud, J. (1998) 'Film audiences', in J. Hill and P. Gibson (eds) *The Oxford guide to film studies*. Oxford: Oxford University Press, pp. 202–211.

Grossberg, L. (1992) 'Is there a fan in the house? The affective sensibility of fandom', in L. Lewis (ed) *The adoring audience — fan culture and popular media*). London: Routledge, pp. 50–65.

—— (1997) 'Replacing popular culture' in S. Redhead with D. Wynne and J. O'Connor (eds) *The clubcultures reader — readings in popular cultural studies*. Oxford: Blackwell, pp. 217–237.

Guttman, A. (1986) *Sports spectators*. New York: Columbia University Press.

Hall, S. (1996) 'Introduction: who needs "identity"?', in S. Hall and P. du Gay (eds) *Questions of cultural identity*. London: Sage, pp. 1–17.

Harrington, C. L. and Bielby, D. D. (1995) *Soap fans — pursuing pleasure and making meaning in everyday life*. Philadelphia: Temple University Press.

Harrison, T. (1996) 'Interview with Henry Jenkins', in T. Harrison, S. Projansky, K. A. Ono, and E. R. Helford (eds) *Enterprise zones — critical positions on Star Trek*. Boulder, Colorado: Westview Press, pp. 259–278.

Harrison, T., Projansky, S., Ono, K. A., and Helford, E. R. (1996) (eds) *Enterprise zones — critical positions on Star Trek*. Boulder, Colorado: Westview Press.

Haynes, R. (1993) 'Every man(?) a football artist: Football writing and masculinity' in S. Redhead (ed) *The passion and the fashion — football fandom in the new Europe*. Aldershot: Avery, pp. 55–76.

—— (1995) *The football imagination: The rise of football fanzine culture*. Aldershot: Arena.

Heide, M. J. (1995) *Television culture and women's lives — thirtysomething and the contradictions of gender*. Philadelphia: University of Pennsylvania Press.

Helford, E. R. (1996) '"A part of myself no man should see" — reading Captain Kirk's multiple masculinities', in T. Harrison, S. Projansky, K. A. Ono, and E. R. Helford (eds) *Enterprise zones — critical positions on Star Trek*. Boulder, Colorado: Westview Press pp. 10–31.

Hogg, M. and Vaughn, G. (1995) *Social psychology: An introduction*. Hemel Hempstead: Harvester Wheatsheaf.

Jenkins, H. (1988) 'Star Trek rerun, reread, rewritten: Fan writing as textual poaching', *Critical Studies in Mass Communication*, Vol. 5, No 2: pp. 85–107.

Jenkins, H. (1991) 'Star Trek rerun, reread, rewritten: Fan writing as textual poaching', in C. Penley, E. Lyon, L. Spigel, and J. Bergstrom (eds) *Close encounters — film, feminism, and science fiction*. Minneapolis: University of Minnesota Press, pp. 171–203.

———— (1992) *Textual poachers — television fans and participatory culture*. London: Routledge.

Jenkins, H. and Tulloch, J. (1995) 'Beyond the Star Trek phenomenon: Reconceptualizing the science fiction audience', in J. Tulloch and H. Jenkins (eds) *Science fiction audiences*. London: Routledge.

Jenson, J. (1992) 'Fandom as pathology: The consequences of characterization', in L. Lewis (ed) *The adoring audience — fan culture and popular media*. London: Routledge, pp. 9–29.

Joseph-Witham, H. (1996) *Star Trek fans and costume art*. Jackson: University Press of Mississippi.

King, A. (1997) 'The lads: Masculinity and the new consumption of football', *Sociology*, Vol. 31, No.2: pp. 329–346.

Lee, A. and Zeiss, C. (1980) 'Behavioural commitment to the role of sport consumer: an exploratory analysis', *Sociology and Social Research*, Vol. 64, No. 3: pp. 405–419.

Lewis, L. (1992) 'Introduction' in L. Lewis (ed) *The adoring audience — fan culture and popular media*. London: Routledge, pp. 1–6.

Livingstone, S. (1994) 'Watching talk: gender and engagement in the viewing of audience discussion programmes', *Media, Culture and Society*, Vol. 16, No. 3: pp. 429–447.

McPherson, B. (1975) 'Socialisation into the role of sports consumer: A theory and causal model', *Canadian Review of Sociology and Anthropology* Vol. 13, No. 2: pp. 165–177.

McQuail, D. (1997) *Audience analysis*. London: Sage.

Madrigal, R. (1995) 'Cognitive and affective determinants of fan satisfaction with sporting event attendance', *Journal of Leisure Research*, Vol. 27, No 3: pp. 205–227.

Mayne, J. (1993) *Cinema and spectatorship*, London: Routledge.

———— (1997) 'L.A. Law and prime-time feminism', in C. Brunsdon, J. D'Acci and L. Spigel (eds) *Feminist television criticism — a reader*. Oxford: Clarendon Press, pp. 84–97.

Messner, M. A. and Sabo, D. F. (1990) 'Introduction: Towards a critical feminist reappraisal of sport, men, and the gender order', in M. A. Messner and D. F. Sabo (eds) *Sport, men and the gender order — critical feminist perspectives*. Champaign: Human Kinetics, pp. 1–18.

Moore, S. (1993) *Interpreting audiences – the ethnography of media consumption*. London: Sage.

Mulvey, L. (1975) 'Visual pleasure and narrative cinema', *Screen*, Vol. 16, No. 3: pp. 6–18.

Murrell, A., and Dietz, B. (1992) 'Fan support of sports teams: The effect of a common group identity', *Journal of Sport and Exercise Psychology*, Vol. 14: pp. 28–39.

Nash, R. (1997) 'Research note: Concept and method in researching the football crowd', *Leisure Studies* Vol. 16: pp. 127–131.

Neale, S. (1993) 'Prologue: masculinity as spectacle — reflections on men and mainstream cinema', in S. Cohan and I.R. Hark (eds) *Screening the male — exploring masculinities in Hollywood cinema*. London: Routledge, pp. 9–20.

Nightingale, V. (1997) *Studying audiences — the shock of the real*. London: Routledge.

Oakes, P., and Turner, J. (1980) 'Social categorisation and inter-group behaviour: Does minimal inter-group discrimination make social identity more positive?', *European Journal of Social Psychology*, Vol. 10: pp. 295–301.

Penley, C. (1991) 'Introduction' in C. Penley, E. Lyon, L. Spigel, and J. Bergstrom (eds) *Close encounters —film, feminism, and science fiction*. Minneapolis: University of Minnesota Press, p. vii–xi.

———— (1997) *NASA/TREK — Popular science and sex in America*. London: Verso.

Pooley, J. (1978) *The sport fan: A social psychology of misbehaviour*. Calgary: CAPHER Sociology of Sport Monograph Series.

Press, A. L. (1990) 'Class, gender and the female viewer: women's responses to Dynasty', in *M. Brown (ed) Television and women's culture — the politics of the popular*. London Sage, pp. 158–180.

Pribram, E. D. (1988) 'Introduction' in E.D. Pribram (ed) *Female spectators — looking at film and television*. London: Verso, pp. 1–11.

Projansky, S. (1996) 'When the body speaks — Deanna Troi's tenuous authority and the rationalization of federation superiority in Star Trek: The Next Generation rape narratives', in T. Harrison, S. Projansky, K. A. Ono, and E. R. Helford (eds) *Enterprise zones — critical positions on Star Trek*. Boulder, Colorado: Westview Press, pp. 33–50.

Rowe, D. (1995) 'Big defence: Sport and hegemonic masculinity', in A. Tomlinson (ed) *Gender, sport and leisure: Continuities and challenges*. Brighton: CSRC, pp. 123–133.

Sherif, M. (1966) *Group conflict and co-operation: Their social psychology*. London: Routledge and Kegan Paul.

Smith, G., Patterson, B., and Williams, T. (1981) 'A profile of the deeply committed male sports fan', *Arena* Vol. 5, No. 2: pp. 26–44.

SNCCFR. (1995, 1996) *F.A Premier League surveys.* Leicester: Sir Norman Chester Centre for Football Research, University of Leicester.

Stacey, J. (1994) *Star gazing: Hollywood cinema and female spectatorship.* London: Routledge.

Stebbins, R. (1992) *Amateurs, professionals, and serious leisure.* Montreal: McGill-Queens University Press.

Tajfel, H. (1982) 'Social psychology of inter-group relations', *Annual Review of Psychology* Vol. 33: pp. 1–39.

Tajfel, H. and Turner, J. (1986) 'The social identity theory of inter-group behaviour', in Worchel, S. and Austin, W. (eds) *Psychology of inter-group relations.* Chicago: Nelson Hall, pp. 7–24.

Taylor, Lord Justice (1990) *The Hillsborough Stadium disaster: Final report.* London: HMSO.

Theberge, N. (1994) 'Towards a feminist alternative to sport as a male preserve', in S. Birrell and C. L. Cole (eds) *Women, sport, and culture.* Champaign: Human Kinetics, pp. 181–192.

Thomas, L. (1997) 'In love with Inspector Morse', in C. Brunsdon, J. D'Acci and L. Spigel (eds) *Feminist television criticism — a reader.* Oxford: Clarendon Press, pp. 184–204.

Tomlinson, A. (1983) 'Introduction' in A. Tomlinson (ed) *Explorations in football culture* (LSA Publication No. 19). Eastbourne: Leisure Studies Association, pp. 1–11.

Tulloch, J. (1990) *Television drama — agency, audience and myth.* London: Routledge.

Tulloch, J. and Jenkins, H. (1995) *Science fiction audiences.* London: Routledge.

Turner, J. (1982) 'Towards a cognitive redefinition of the social group', in H. Tajfel (ed) *Social identity and inter-group relations* 15—40. London: Academic Press.

Turner, G. (1993) *Film and social practice* (2nd edition). London: Routledge.

Waddington, I., Dunning, E. and Murphy, P. (1996) 'Research note: Surveying the social composition of football crowds', *Leisure Studies* Vol. 15: pp. 209–214.

Wann, D. and Branscombe, N. (1993) 'Sports fans: measuring degree of identification with their team', *International Journal of Sports Psychology* Vol. 24: pp. 1–17.

Wann, D. and Dolan, T. (1994) 'Influence of spectator's identification on evaluation of past, present and future performance of a sports team', *Perceptual and Motor Skills,* Vol. 78: pp. 547–552.

Wann, D. and Hamlet, M. (1995) 'Author and subject gender in sport research', *International Journal of Sport Psychology,* Vol. 26: pp. 225–232.

Wann, D. and Schrader, M. (1996) 'An analysis of the stability of sport team identification', *Perceptual and Motor Skills*, Vol. 82: pp. 322–323.

Wann, D. Tucker, K. and Schrader, M. (1996) 'An exploratory examination of the factors influencing the origination, continuation and cessation of identification with sports teams', *Perceptual and Motor Skills*, Vol. 82 pp. 995–1001.

Wearing, B. (1998) *Leisure and feminist theory*. London: Sage.

Wenner, L.A. (1998) 'Playing the MediaSport game', in L. A. Wenner (ed) *MediaSport* London: Routledge, pp. 3–13.

Wenner, L.A. and Gantz, W. (1989) 'The audience experience with sports on television', in L. A. Wenner (ed) *Media, sports and society*. Newbury Park: Sage, pp. 242–269.

——— (1998) 'Watching sports on television: audience experience, gender, fanship, and marriage', in L. A. Wenner (ed) *Media, sports and society*. Newbury Park: Sage, pp. 223–252.

Whannel, G. (1998a) 'Individual stars and collective identities in media sport', in M. Roche (ed) *Sport, popular culture and identity*. Aachen: Meyer and Meyer Verlag, pp. 23–36.

Whannel, G. (1998b) 'Reading the sports media audience', in. L. A. Wenner (ed) *MediaSport*. London: Routledge, pp. 221–232.

Widdecombe, S. and Wooffitt, R. (1995) *The language of youth subcultures*. Hemel Hempstead: Harvester Wheatsheaf.

Williams, J. (1994) *English football stadia after Hillsborough*. Leicester: Sir Norman Chester Centre for Football Research, University of Leicester.

Williams, J. (1996) 'Surveying the social composition of football crowds: a reply to Waddington, Dunning and Murphy', *Leisure Studies*, Vol. 15: pp. 215–219.

Williams, J. and Woodhouse, J. (1991) 'Can play, will play? Women and Football in Britain', in J. Williams and S. Wagg (eds) *British football and social change*. Leicester: Leisure University Press.

Woodhouse, J. (1990) *A national survey of female football fans*. Leicester: Sir Norman Chester Centre for Football Research.

Van Zoonen, L. (1994) *Feminist media studies*. London: Sage.

Zillman, D. and Paulus, P. (1993) 'Spectators: Reactions to sporting events and effects on athletic performance', in R. Singer, M. Murphey and L. Tennant (eds) *Handbook of research on sport psychology*. New York: Macmillan, pp. 600–619.

Game, Set and Match: Gender Bias in Television Coverage of Wimbledon 1994

Lesley Fishwick and Kirsty Leach

University of Northumbria, Wynne-Jones Centre (UK)

Introduction

As the millennium fast approaches there is little doubt that women's sport has won some important battles and made progress towards equality. In this respect, tennis has been a front runner not least for the famous victory of Billie Jean King over Bobby Riggs in the media hyped battle of the sexes in 1973. In general, women's professional tennis has grown greatly over the last 20 years in terms of expansion in the number of tournaments, prize money, and sponsorship. As a result athletes have emerged as media figures in a sport in which men and women compete for attention (Wagner, 1994). Herein lies the rain cloud on the tennis horizon for women. Competing for resources, especially lucrative television deals may be one of the biggest battles yet. So far the forecast is not good for fair weather ahead.

Long range forecast

The relationship between sport and the media is not a modern day phenomenon. Since organised sport has existed the media has taken full advantage of its cultural popularity (Birrell and Loy, 1981). Although debates abound whether this is a mutually beneficial relationship or a parasitic one, the evidence suggests that neither sport nor the media have backed away from the association. The entanglement is so strong that sports administrators view the media as perhaps the major determinant of the futures of different sports and sports people (McKay and Rowe, 1987). Initially the outlook looks good as media coverage has finally given visibility to women athletes. Steffi Graf, Martina Navratilova, Martina Hingis and

31

Chris Evert are all household names. However, when we examine the actual amount and type of coverage a different picture emerges as the future of women's sport appears to be stagnating as researchers find that women athletes do not fare well in terms of either the amount of media coverage or the type of coverage.

The majority of studies examine the sport pages of national newspapers and find that women are vastly under-represented (Klein (1988), Duncan and Hasbrook (1988), Halbert and Latimer (1994)). Researchers such as Duncan (1990) then delve deeper to analyse the images of men and women in sport and capture the way in which camera angles and shot selection sexualise and devalue women's sporting achievement. Similar analyses have opened up a rich vein of inquiry concerning narratives of television sport and the underlying messages given to the audiences.

This vast array of research across media studies, cultural studies and sport sociology documents the subtle and unobtrusive manner in which the media manipulates sporting events. Clarke and Clarke (1982) indicate how television viewers have the illusionary impression of watching an event impartially first hand, when in actual fact the images are filtered through an array of choices of camera angles and commentators interpretations. Creedon (1994) notes how the media selectively impose language and terminology applied to women's sport to provide highly stereotypical views and draws attention to the extensive coverage of the USA women's gymnastic team in terms of little pixies whose bodies are shown in graceful aesthetic motion. Hilliard (1984) found similar descriptors for women tennis players in sport magazines. Kane and Greendorfer (1988) assert that such feminine images represent a modernised attempt by the media to reinforce traditional sex stereotypical images and as such pose no threat to male hegemony. Dewar (1994) goes further to conclude that strong, powerful and talented women whose performances potentially challenge hegemonic representations of the 'weaker' sex are trivialised, marginalised and sexualised in an attempt to diffuse any threat to male power and privilege. A central tenet of much of the research is that trivialisation is one of the key mechanisms which emerges from analysis of sports writing, photography and commentary which undermines women's sporting achievements. Table 1 summarises the main strategies identified by researchers over the last 20 years.

Researchers conclude from the studies summarised in Table 1 that the media communicate a general message that sportsmen are powerful and important, while sportswomen are subordinate and relatively unimportant. Does this message ever vary; for instance, when the media cover a sport such as tennis which is acceptable for both men and women to compete at a professional level in Grand Slam tournaments? Is the message any

Table 1   **Main research strategies in the 1980s and 1990s**

Topic	Mechanism	Researcher
Young Athlete Magazines	• Less coverage for women • Coverage limited to sports such as tennis, figure skating, gymnastics and athletics	Rintala and Birrell 1984
Magazine articles on professional tennis players	• Images confirm sex role stereotypes: pretty, slim and feminine • Framing women as failures more often than males	Hilliard 1984
Sport reports of national newspapers	• Reports on women contain less sport specific information and more on their social and private lives	Klein 1988
Television broadcasts of NCAA Basketball, National Surfing Championships and New York Marathon	• Sports women receive more comments on their physical appearance rather than performance • Ambivalence in the portrayals of sportswomen	Duncan and Hasbrook 1988
Newspaper reports on 1984 and 1988 Summer Olympics	• Women subject to discursive strategies • Juxtaposition of strengths and weaknesses • References to physiological differences between men and women	Lee 1992
Television broadcasts of 1992 Summer Olympic Games	• Gender marking of 'women's athletic events (men's as the norm and women as 'other') • Focus on personalities for women	Higgs and Weiller 1994
Television broadcast of Battle of the Champions (Navratilova versus Connors)	• Mixed messages (positive comment followed by negative comment) • Sportswomen receive less praise • Reference to female athletes as girls or ladies • Calling female athletes by their first names and men by their surnames	Halbert and Latimer 1994
Television broadcast of 1992 Winter Olympic Games	• Condescending descriptors • Compensatory rhetoric • Adolescent ideal • Female athletes as co-operative	Daddario 1994

different in the UK context where a public broadcasting company covers the event? A cursory glance indicates that the BBC give time to the women's and men's tournaments but what if any differences exist in how men's and women's tennis is presented to the public?

The subtlety of the potential bias in commentary requires in depth analysis to capture how the media are a potent force in the ideological struggle over sport as they shape people's views, attitudes and beliefs about the men's and women's game. The British Tennis Open, Wimbledon seeped in tradition and prestige provides an ideal opportunity to examine the linguistic construction and reconstruction of gender difference in the television narrative of Wimbledon 1994.

Method

Rationale

Wimbledon was chosen as the sporting event for several reasons. Acceptance of tennis as a appropriate sport for females to play (Metheney, 1972); females can retain true 'feminine' values such as glamour, elegance and grace (Boutlier and SanGiovanni, 1983). Males and females compete alongside each other for equivalent titles and therefore comparisons of their treatment by the media can be made. The large amount of media coverage given to this event (which many players regard as the most prestigious of all the Grand Slam tournaments); over the Wimbledon fortnight BBC1 and BBC2 broadcast live each afternoon and round up with a highlight show every evening.

Content analysis of television narrative

The data were collected from the British Broadcasting Corporation (BBC) coverage of the 1994 Wimbledon tournament. Each day coverage lasted from 12 pm to 4 pm BBC1 and from 3 pm to 6.30 pm BBC2. Over thirty hours of Wimbledon coverage (BBC1 and BBC2) are analysed. Commentators match comments are transcribed verbatim and transferred onto NUDIST qualitative database. The study utilised both qualitative and quantitative dimensions of content analysis of the narrative used by commentators. Such content analysis holds the means to examine the content and the message of the media and, as Rintala and Birrell (1984) note, the underlying assumption is that the commentators values, attitudes and interpretation of the events influence the message they produce.

Quantitative analysis

A table was devised (Figure 1) of categories to code both the sex of the commentators and the type of comments in a quantitative fashion. The categories were derived from themes in the literature. Specific matches were selected for the quantitative analysis and the sample included all of the televised games of the top 4 male players (1. Peter Sampras; 2. Michel Stich; 3. Stefan Edberg; 4. Goran Ivanisevic) and female players (1. Stefi Graf; 2. Arancha Sanchez-Vicario; 3. Conchita Martinez; 4. Martina Navratilova). The purpose of this analysis was to identify trends which where then analysed much more in-depth in the qualitative data. For each match involving one of the top four seeds a table was completed containing the

Men/Women; Match_____ Round_____

Comments	male commentator:	female commentator:
Positive:		
• fitness/athleticism		
• play		
• misc.		
Negative:		
• fitness/athleticism		
• play		
• misc.		
Victories		
Defeats		
First name calling		
Emotions		
Character flaws		
Beauty and fashion		
Patronising		

Figure 1　　**Table for coding of commentary**

comments for the seeded player, noting the number of references that corresponded to each of the identified categories (Leach, 1995).

Qualitative analysis

Qualitative analysis is the subjective interpretation of the narrative. This involved an in-depth reading of the narrative text of the television commentary. In a deductive fashion, the initial codes followed the themes identified from the review of literature and also used in the quantitative analysis. Further analysis followed in an inductive fashion as further codes and themes emerged from an open-ended analysis of the television narrative or text. Questions identified by Duncan and Hasbrook (1988) guided this search for themes (often not explicit) and underlying meaning:

> What is being given special attention in this text?
> Is there a particular emphasis or neglect of any feature of the text?
> Are there contradictory messages or themes?
> What are the text's unspoken or subtle assumptions and how do they manifest themselves? (Duncan and Hasbrook, 1988)

In this way the focus of the analysis is not only on what is being said but how it is being said and the emphasis is on the fixation of the discourse via its meaning. The overall aim was to characterise the type of commentary used for each of the men and women's games. A further strength of the analysis lies in the combination of the qualitative and quantitative modes.

Triangulation of data

Much has been written over the comparative merits of quantitative and qualitative approaches to research. There is some debate that qualitative research is the antithesis of more traditional approaches (Thomas and Nelson, 1996). However, there is a growing appreciation that by combining the two methodologies in terms of triangulation of the data provides an in-depth analysis of the phenomenon in question (for the present study — the television narrative). Quantitative analysis focuses on examining components of the phenomenon and in this case this included quantifying the general types of comments. This simple quantitative counting reveals the extent of the patterns, whereas the qualitative analysis seeks to understand meaning and focuses on the 'essence' of the tennis narrative, especially exploring the logic of 'difference' between the men's and women's games. As Denzin (1978) notes, the different methods of observation reveal different aspects of empirical reality.

Results

Centre Court — number one seed — men's tennis

By far the clearest message that emerges from the Wimbledon commentary is that men's tennis is far superior to women's tennis. Women's tennis is not judged in it's own right as an autonomous entity but almost always in comparison to men. Messner (1993) has termed this asymmetrical gender marking, that is the process whereby a male sporting event is treated as the norm, whereas the women are marked as 'ōther'. This occurs in subtle ways such as referring to the women's final as the 'Ladies Final', whilst the men's final is simply called 'The Final'. Also this treatment of men's tennis as the only standard of excellence frequently occurs through constant direct comparisons between women's tennis and the men's game:

> "Graf really has the best forehand in the game ... the women's game that is. I don't think it would be quite so effective against the likes of Sampras."

> "She can't cope with these late arrivals at the net ... it's a very good tactic, it's one John McEnroe often used."

> "Martina's a natural serve volleyer, which is very unusual in women's tennis."

Several times during a women's match the commentators would recall a similar incident in a men's game or mention an example of a famous male tennis player from the past. The reverse never happened when commentating on the men's game. The message relayed to the audience is that the male athlete is dominant and this constantly undermines the women's game. The unstated "fact" which underlies the discourse is that if you put the men's number one and women's number one on any surface, the man would win. In this way, tennis is reduced to a game about strength and power. Tennis commentary captures how the sport discourse presents as "natural" the debatable issues of what is the essence of particular sports in terms of defining characteristics (e.g. complexity and variety of skills required). In one instance, the commentators noted how the current debate over the domination of the serve in the men's game overlooks the complexity and variety of skill in the game and specifically mention the other skills required of the men's clay court specialists. Even their own 'essence' has contradictions as the same arguments about tactical awareness and strategies involved in the long rallies as opposed to just service power are never mentioned for the women's game. Overall, the commentators implicitly compare the women's and men's game and assert that the men's game is the best and most dominant. In this way commentators reduce the issues surrounding skill and talent to a debate about men versus women rather than judging the women's game in its own right.

Number One Court: girls and ladies

Another frequent demeaning descriptor used to describe the women athletes as 'girls', whereas male athletes were never referred to as 'boys'. Examples include:

> "Clare Taylor is a promising young girl."

> "Neither [of the] girls are playing well."

> "Both girls started with a double fault."

In the above examples, the term 'girls' is used in a descriptive fashion which researchers such as Richardson (1993) suggest implies immaturity and incompetence. In other cases, the term has a patronising element which trivialises the players accomplishments. For example, after a particularly gruelling ground stroke rally played to the limits, the only comment from the commentary team was somewhat demeaning:

> "Well, a little attempt at exhibition tennis there from the girls. Very nice."

In a similar vein, the descriptor of women tennis players as ladies, although innocuous on the surface, has a derogatory tone in terms of sporting achievement. This description of 'ladies' is traditionally bound up with notions of appropriate behaviour and of being 'feminine'. Halbert and Latimer (1994) put it more strongly and suggest that the term 'lady' implies helplessness, elegance and a lack of athletic abilities. Such commentary trivialises the women tennis players and their performances. Examples include:

> "Here we go. A ladies match."

> "Martina — the greatest lady player of all time."

> "Miyagi is not a tall lady."

Such language reinforces existing ambivalence about women's sport and women athletes. This is further reinforced by the differential way that commentators refer to the players in terms of first names or surnames.

On first name terms

The statistics in this section are overwhelming: the top four seeded women received a total of 589 references to their first names, while the top four men received a mere 12 references to their first names. This result needs some qualification, given that the 1994 Wimbledon was Navratilova's last appearance in this championship resulting in particular media attention. One of the many matches which illustrates this point was the semi-final between Navratilova and Fernandez. Navratilova was referred to as 'Martina' a staggering 78 times throughout the duration of the match. In a corresponding men's semi-final between Ivanesivic and Becker, Ivanesevic was never referred to by his first name, Goran. Interestingly, on one occasion during another match the umpire set the tone by announcing that it was "Martina to serve" (although this never happened for a men's match). Although the specific championship may have skewed the result somewhat the audience still hear the overriding tendency for commentators to call female players only by their first names.

In general language usage, the use of the surname is more formal and respectful. Correspondingly, the findings suggest that reference to the surname gives males more status and covertly presents this message to the viewer. Halbert and Latimer (1994) findings were similar on their study on woman tennis players. They coined this phenomenon 'gendered hierarchy of naming' and concluded that this practice undermines women's athletic participation. Referring formally to men by using their surname, and informally to women by using the first name establishes a dominate/ subordinate relationship and subtly asserts that female participation and achievements are inferior to those of males. There are many other ways in which this trivialization is transmitted to viewers, in terms of how the commentators frame success and failure for men and women, and in terms of how they allocate criticism and praise.

Mixed Doubles: slow to praise yet quick to criticise the ladies!

Differences in the amount of praise and criticism given to men and women players is another obvious way in which commentators create gender inequities. In general, women receive more negative comments and less positive comments than their male counterparts. Using Navratilova and Ivanesivic (both seeded 4) in two of their matches proves an interesting comparison:

3rd Round (both players won)

Navratilova:	15 positive remarks	9 negative remarks
Ivanisevic:	35 positive remarks	2 negative comments

Final (both players lost)

Navratilova:	16 positive remarks	22 negative remarks
Ivanisevic:	21 positive remarks	1 negative comments

Again, the quantitative data show the trend and are an illustrative example. What is also clear when the qualitative analysis is taken into account is that the commentators often relay mixed messages when describing the women's matches as a positive comment is often regularly followed by a negative comment:

> "Linda is hitting some great shots but I do not think her mental attitude is consistent enough."

> "An excellent serve by Mary Joe and one feels she could have made more advantage of it."

> "A great shot there from Martina, that should give her some confidence after the two previous poor shots."

There is much less evidence of this type of narrative throughout the men's game. Certainly this mixture of praise then criticism sends an ambiguous message to the audience which undermines women's tennis. The message, however, is certainly not mixed when we analyse the type of situations which appear to warrant praise and criticism, as this follows gendered paths. Praise for the women often focuses on stereotypical 'feminine' qualities:

> "Graf has such elegance on court."

> "McNeil has gorgeous movements. So aesthetically pleasing."

> "GeGe plays a very attractive game. Serves beautifully, volleys very pretty."

Adjectives such as graceful, elegant, beautiful, pretty and flowing are commonly used to describe tennis strokes made by the women. In sharp contrast the praise for men contain very different connotations:

> "These missiles are thundering past him now ... perhaps he should dig a trench."

> "Spectacular and assertive tennis."

"Ivanisevic has such power, he loves the aggressive game."

Adjectives such as power, aggression, assertive, brutal, commanding and intimidating are regularly spoken during the men's game and create a more domineering impression of the matches. The positive comments in the narrative concentrates on male dominance, strength and power. While the commentators do occasionally indicate the power of some of the women players, such as Lindsay Davenport, they often then counter this by saying that she does not move very well on the court. Also, as well as commenting on skills the commentators are much more likely to mention personality aspects when discussing the women:

"Aranchez ... a very busy player, very bubbly personality always seems to enjoy her matches."

"Julia's not the most outgoing of people .... Meridith has a very well rounded personality."

"Mary Jo ... well those little knee bends seem to do the trick."

In this way the commentators reinforce stereotypical sex role expectations even within competitive sport. Similar framing occurs when criticising the players. Women are often described as having too much of those 'feminine' qualities in terms of characteristics such as emotions:

"Pam has had matches where she has been somewhat emotionally demonstrative."

"Neiland .... has potential but she does tend to get a little bit excited when she gets ahead."

"Gee-Gee ... the exuberance and excitement of the day, she's running out of that enthusiasm."

This ploy of mentioning the "disadvantage" of uncontrollable emotions was most clear in the final as Navratilova lost. The fact that it was her last appearance encouraged the commentators to characterise her as a player shackled by her emotions and 16 references were made to her emotional state with comments such as:

"Martina is struggling with her emotions."

"I wonder if the emotion is all too much for her?"

"Has Martina got enough control over her emotion to get through here?"

Although not a perfect comparison as it was not his last appearance, in relation to Ivanisevic, who did lose the final and is known as a 'volatile' player, no references were made to his emotions during the match. So again, commentators note the emotions of the women players to a greater extent than the men's, and this in turn points to vulnerability and devalues the women's play.

Another tactic is to criticise the women in terms of their lack of aggression, lack of concentration or lack of stamina. So in addition to being criticised more often, the women are also framed as lacking essential qualities, not quite having what it takes to win is the underlying message.

> "Pam is not as fit as she used to be, and she has had quite a few injuries."

> "Lynsey Davenport doesn't move particularly well but I am sure people will be working on that aspect of her game."

> "Durie is over 6 foot and fitness doesn't come easily to her."

Overall the commentators are much more likely to criticise the women and often in a very patronising manner especially when a point is lost:

> "Oh dear just a little bit over anxious as she knows she has to come to the net."

> "That was rather a pity, it was an opportunity but Jo didn't see it coming quickly enough."

> "That's a shame, she did everything right but get it over the net."

The last examples also indicate that winning and losing overall elicits very different commentary for the men and women's matches.

Winners and losers: those two impostors are not treated the same

Even when women are successful, commentators frame these victories in a very different light. Commentators attributed some of the women's successes to luck or chance, whereas for men the commentators framed the victories in terms of the player's power and domination:

women's victories	*men's victories*
"an accident"	"total domination"
"greater experience winning through"	"supremacy"

"managing to control her emotions"   "devastating"

"failings of her opponent"   "an exhibition of remarkable power"

In a similar vein, losers were not treated equally either. One of the best comparisons for this was provided in the first round as both Steffi Graf and Michael Stich lost unexpectedly. Graf was said to be "emotionally unstable", "not sufficiently prepared", "preoccupied by personal problems" and "suffering from a lack of decent competition". Stich's loss was attributed to "being very unlucky" as "he had played a fine match but was overpowered by a greater player on the day". This is a general tendency and the message when the women lose is "she hasn't had the best of luck, she faced a tough opponent". The different framing of women's victories and defeats again serves to trivialise their success, whereas this rarely if ever happens for the men.

Wimbledon round-up: game, set and match

The major patterns emerging from the data include asymmetrical gender marking (treating male tennis as the norm) and trivialisation and marginalisation of women's achievements. The theme during the men's matches is often one of a victorious battle of skill and power, whereas for the women's matches the television narrative is often patronising, overly critical and focuses on negative aspects of emotional troubles and weak opponents. In this way, the commentators shape the preferred text for audiences and thereby shape viewers' interpretation of men and women's tennis. Television narrative influences how people make sense of sport and the present study clearly indicates that women's status as athletes continues to be challenged. This confirms previous findings which conclude that sport commentary helps construct and legitimise hegemonic masculinity thereby reproducing gender relations in society (see Duncan, 1986; Duncan and Hasbrook, 1988; Duncan et al., 1990; Harris and Hills, 1993; and Weiller and Higgs, 1994). The linguistic analysis of the Wimbledon commentary emphasises the importance of language and representation as the principle ingredient of any discourse and highlights the power of the media in shaping the construction of gender differences. Even the hallowed centre court of Wimbledon, for all its recent refurbishment and media centre, remains very much a male preserve.

References

Birrell, S. and Loy, J. (1981) 'Media Sport: Hot and cool', in Loy, J. and B.D. McPherson (eds) *Sport, Culture and Society: A Reader in the Sociology of Sport*. MA.: Addison-Wesley, pp. 296–307.

Boutilier, M. and SanGiovanni, L. (1983) *The sporting woman*. Champaign, IL: Human Kinetics.

Clarke, A. and J. Clarke (1982) 'Highlights and action replays: Ideology, sport and the media', in J. Hargreaves (ed) Sport, Culture and Society. London: Routledge and Kegan Paul, pp. 62–87.

Creedon, P. (1994) *Women, media and sport: Changing gender values*. London: Sage, pp. 2–28.

Denzin, N. (1978) *The research act:* A theoretical introduction to sociological methods. New York: McGraw and Hill.

Duncan, M. (1990) 'Sports photographs and sexual difference: Images of women and men in the 1984 and 1988 Olympic Games', *Sociology of Sport Journal*, 7: pp. 22–43.

Duncan, M. and C. Hasbrook (1988) 'Denial of power in televised women's sports', *Sociology of Sport Journal*, 5(1): pp. 1–21.

Halbert, C. and Latimer, M. (1994) 'Battling gendered language used by sports commentators in a televised coed tennis competition', *Sociology of Sport Journal*, 11: pp. 298–307.

Higgs, C. and K. Weiller (1994) 'Gender bias and the 1992 summer Olympic games: An analysis of television coverage', *Journal of Sport and Social Issues*, 18: pp. 234–246.

Hilliard, D. (1984) 'Media images of male and female professional athletes: An interpretive analysis of magazine articles', *Sociology of Sport Journal*, 1: pp. 251–262.

Klein, M. (1992) 'Women in the discourse of sports reports', *International Review of Sociology of Sport*, 23.

Leach, K. (1995) On first name terms: To what extent is there gender bias in the media's reporting of Wimbledon 1994. Unpublished undergraduate thesis, University of Northumbria.

McKay, J. and Rowe, D. (1987) 'Ideology and the media and Australian Sport', *Sociology of Sport Journal*, 4 (3): 258–273.

Metheney, E. (1972). 'Symbolic forms of movement: the feminine image of sports', in M. Hart (ed) *Sport in the sociocultural Process*. Dubuque, IA, pp. 277–290.

Rintala, J. and S. Birrell (1984) 'Fair treatment for the active female: A content analysis of *Young Athlete* magazine', *Sociology of Sport Journal*, 1: 231–250.

Are Your Kids Safe?: Media Representations of Sexual Abuse in Sport

Caroline Fusco
University of Manitoba (Canada)

Sandra Kirby
University of Winnipeg (Canada)

LIBRARY, UNIVERSITY COLLEGE CHESTER

Introduction: hockey, masculinity, media and dominant discourses of sexuality

> I thought I was living in Ancient Greece ...
> (Graham James, convicted child sexual abuser)

> Hockey is not just the national pastime in Canada: in many respects Canadians will tell you, it is Canada. The essence of hockey — ruggedness, brute strength and guile on ice — is sometimes seen as a macho modern manifestation of Canadians' long-ago beginnings as trappers and explorers trying to tame their harsh environments. (DePalma, *The New York Times*, 16 January, 1997: p. A10)

Are your kids safe if their coach thinks he or she is living in Ancient Greece? This paper analyses the homophobia and heterosexism in the media reporting of a nationally (Canada) known case of child sexual abuse. Coach Graham James, an award winning Canadian junior ice hockey coach sentenced to three and one half years in prison for the sexual abuse of two male players in his charge. We show that, through content analysis of print media coverage of the James case, there was evidence of manifest and latent homophobia in some of the articles. There are also signs that some media and sport personnel appear confused about terms such as sexual predation and sexual orientation, and also hold very stereotypical notions of heterosexuality and homosexuality.

As Canada's national pastime, ice hockey has enjoyed a "cherished status," (Monchuk, *The Globe and Mail*, 26 December, 1997: p. A7); it is a "deeply Canadian ritual, a religion ... a balm for the soul" (DePalma, *The New York Times*, 16 January, 1997: p. A10). Ice hockey in Canadian culture does not hold its cherished status just from the game per se, but from its historical links with Canadian masculinity. As an organized sport, it developed as a distinctly masculine subculture and male preserve, and has "come to occupy the place it holds in Canadian culture in part because it provides a public platform for celebrating a very traditional masculine ideal" (Gruneau and Whitson, 1993: p. 190). This "very traditional ideal" has been based on a "specific model of aggressive masculinity" (Gruneau and Whitson: p. 191), and it is this that has given the ice hockey subculture its macho image.

This is no different from many other sports which, historically, have been labeled as male domains and where athleticism has been equated with masculinity (Birrell, 1988; Crosset, 1990; Dunning, 1994; Kidd, 1990; Willis, 1982). In fact sports, traditionally, have been sites for the construction and reconstruction of masculine patriarchal hegemony and the naturalizing of men's abilities. (Boutilier and San Giovanni, 1983; Bryson, 1987; Hall, 1988; Kane, 1995; Lenskyj, 1987, 1991).

In the masculine world of ice hockey, the quintessential Canadian sport, playing in the National Hockey League (NHL) as a professional athlete is the dream of many (male) youths in Canada. In order for young boys to achieve this dream they must become involved in junior hockey which has been defined as a "rite of passage for Canadian [male] athletes who wish to play professional hockey" (Lapointe, *The New York Times*, February 23, 1997: p. 3). Junior hockey has become a way to initiate young boys into the realm of the masculine subculture of hockey as well as developing the skills they need to play at top levels (Gruneau and Whitson, 1993). The importance of hockey in Canada is evidenced by the fact that:

> There are 3, 000 arenas in the country ... That gives Canada three times as many arenas as hospitals. In a population of 30 million more than 4.2 million are involved in hockey as players, coaches, officials, administrators or volunteers. In youth league play alone there are more than 480, 000 youngsters from 4 to age 20. (DePalma, *The New York Times*, 16 January, 1997: p. A10)

From these male youth leagues come the players who will move into minor hockey where potential future professionals are identified and groomed (Gruneau and Whitson, 1993). In terms of the subculture that surrounds it and the type of skills that are required, Major Junior League (MJL) hockey in Canada somewhat mirrors the NHL (Gruneau and Whitson, 1993). For boys who are involved in this subculture:

> ... minor-hockey arenas have been "fields of dreams" where Canadian boys have tried to emulate their favorite stars .... minor hockey and junior hockey have also provided opportunities for generations of Canadian men who remain staunch believers in the values of introducing young males into the codes of masculine behaviour that have been defining features of their own lives. (Gruneau and Whitson: p. 169)

We would suggest that these "codes of behaviour" shared and understood by "hockey men" not only include a particular idealized notion of masculinity but one of masculine heterosexuality. Messner (1996) suggests that, historically, hegemonic masculinity has been reconstructed in sport in order to assert clear links between masculinity and heterosexuality. There has been a proliferation of work to demonstrate that hierarchies of sexuality exist among men in sport (Gruneau and Whitson, 1993; Klein, 1990; McConnell, 1990; Messner, 1996; Messner and Sabo, 1994; Pronger, 1990). In North American society representations of (hetero)sexual identities and ways of being masculine in sport have normally been rewarded. These forms of (hetero) hegemonic masculinity (Connell, 1990) have been maintained through heterosexism and homophobia in sport, and have assisted in naturalizing and (re)producing (hetero)sexual hierarchies. Kimmel (1994) states:

> Homophobia is a central organizing principle in our cultural definition of manhood. Homophobia is more that the irrational fear of gay men, more than the fear that we might be perceived as gay... Homophobia is the fear that other men will unmask us, emasculate us, reveal to us and the world that we do not measure up, that we are not real men. (p. 131)

Consequently the fear of being a "sissy" dominates North American cultural definitions of masculinity and because masculinity must be proved homosexuals become the 'other' against which heterosexual men project their identities (Kimmel, 1994). There have been several studies that have demonstrated that in most (heterosexual) male sports subcultures, marginalization and vilification of homosexuality takes place (Klein, 1990; McConnell, 1990; Wheatley, 1994; White and Vagi, 1990). Homosexuals and homosexuality have been mocked either through overt songs and performances (Wheatley, 1994; White and Vagi, 1990) or through ritualized homosexual and homophobic hazings, (Robinson, 1998). This vilification allows heterosexual males to act and be "supermasculine" (Wheatley, 1994). This "supermasculinity" in conjunction with homophobia "functions in the socialization of males to establish a standard permissible and prohibited behaviour and values" in sport (Klein, 1990: p. 132). Thus in male sports a "homo/hetero hierarchy" (Fuss, 1991) is maintained where heterosexuality is continually privileged over homosexuality.

It is suggested here that not only does the privileging of hetero over homosexuality take place in the hypermasculine and hyper(hetero)sexual environment of men's ice hockey, but that it is also extended to the media's portrayal of the Sheldon Kennedy/Graham James sexual abuse case within that sport. The awareness of same-sex abuse in this hypermasculine environment seemed to be a shock to the ice hockey world: "some who revere the macho world of elite hockey took the news like a stick in the gut" (Galloway, *The Winnipeg Free Press*, February 7 1997)[1]. Consequently, we suggest that the discursive practices of the print media framed the story within dominant arrangements of (hetero)/(homo)sexuality.

The basic media rationale is the representation of the world to the reader or viewer. The media represent the world to us, through the use of text, images, sound and in the case of television, visual language and commentary. The power of the media lies in its capacity to 'naturalize' events and the world in ways that may encourage the reader or viewer to receive and uncritically accept the message and meanings it communicates. The role of the mass media in shaping public perceptions of 'reality' in sports has been widely documented (Cantelon and Gruneau, 1988; Davis, 1993; Duncan, 1990; Jackson, 1994; Jhally, 1989; King, 1993; MacNeill, 1988; Messner and Sabo; 1994; Rowe, 1994; Theberge, 1989; Theberge and Cronk, 1986; Wenner, 1989). King (1993) states:

> Newspapers and television in particular produce news, not truth; through frames, values and conventions they actively define, construct, and reproduce images of our society and, using various methods of legitimation, present them as fact. (p. 271)

The news from sport is thus 'mediated' in terms of what meanings are attached to it, what is highlighted, ignored or de-emphasized (Messner and Solomon, 1994). Messner and Solomon suggested that even though media text[2] is an "inherently ideological construct ... it rarely appears so ..." because "meanings are commonly drawn from socially shared (hegemonic) understandings of the world" (p. 54). Other researchers have investigated the social construction of sports images and news and how particular text and images are privileged over others in confirming and reinforcing dominant discourses (Davis, 1993; King, 1993; Rowe, 1994; Therberge, 1989). A question that might be posed is why do the media construct privileged meanings within sports? Lowes (1997) stated:

> Metropolitan daily newspapers, like any other free market enter-prise, sell a product to buyers. (p. 146)

In economic terms, with a concern to create an audience for advertisers, the media have acted "as publicity agents for sports" (Jhally, 1989: p. 80). That the Sheldon Kennedy/Graham James sexual abuse story took place within the context of ice hockey immediately set it apart from other stories of abuse in Canada.

> Harassment in sport — a new issue? With all the press that Graham James ... is getting, one might think this is the first harassment case that has ever been brought forward in the sports community. (Lawrence, *The Vancouver Sun*, 23 January, 1997: p. A2)

Given that the metropolitan newspapers are "saturated with commercial sports ... they are cash cows" (Lowes, 1997: p. 147), the commercial value of this story was evident in that it involved a professional NHL player talking about his experiences in the Major Junior Leagues which in themselves constitute big business sports, (Wong, *The Globe and Mail*, 13 January, 1997). In addition, part of the provision to provide commercial sports is inherently linked to the audience. Lowes (1997) reported that the 'right' sports audience (readers) are "18 to 49-year-old males with disposable income" and the most effective way to attract male readers is to provide extensive coverage of commercial spectator sports ..." (pp. 146–147).

This story had all the 'ingredients' to sell to a male audience, particu-larly a heterosexual male audience, because it involved semi-professional sport, and the sport of ice hockey. This played a role in maintaining the male audience's interest in the story. In addition the 'homophile context' of the story within the hypermasculine and hyper(hetero)sexual context of ice hockey provided the sensationalism to maintain the story's commercial value.

> ... this recent attention ... what was the catalyst? Was it the fact that this type of harassment took place in the sport that holds the most national pride, or is it because it happened to a male athlete ... (Lawrence, *The Vancouver Sun*, 23 January, 1997: p. A2)

Within this context the stories functioned as socially sanctioned gossip sheets for men ... a place where a great deal of conjecture [was] placed upon 'heroes' and events ... (Wenner, 1989: p. 15).

Newspapers and news-gathering are involved in a "process of 'moral evaluation' whereby decisions are made about what acts are out of place, hence newsworthy" (Ericson *et al.*, 1991 in Peelo and Soothill, 1994: p. 17). While defining events as newsworthy the media often structures interpretations of how the audience should understand these events (Theberge, 1989). They do this by encoding meaning in the text; the audience then decode the text and produce meanings (Hall, 1984). The codes, or components of language are often structured to suggest and encourage "preferred meanings," "particular world views" through the use of "dominant or commonly understood and accepted discourses" (Davis, 1993: p. 168). Although the readers have control in reading the text they do not have control over the production of the codes or meanings. Often the structure, the content of the piece, constraints, available evidence, and access to discourses outside the mainstream can act to limit the range of alternative interpretations or readings (Davis, 1993; Jhally, 1989).

> Because the producers consciously or unconsciously have encouraged this type of reading by the content and structure of their texts, these producers are consciously or unconsciously helping to naturalize dominant ideological assumptions. When dominant assumptions are taken for granted, they help produce consent for the status quo. (Davis, 1993: p. 169)

In this paper we present evidence to demonstrate that the media not only acted as a catalyst for exposing sexual abuse in ice hockey but that they often did so within existing dominant arrangements of essentialist notions of sexuality, gender, race, 'otherness', and difference.

Methodology

The goal of this research was to evaluate the nature and scope of homophobia and heterosexism in the print media coverage of the sexual abuse case against Graham James, junior hockey coach in Canada. Because the media coverage was extensive, a content analysis was indicated.

First, we gathered all available related articles published between October 13, 1996 and February 28, 1998 in 22 major newspapers and magazines, including four international publications. Included were 105 articles, 7 cartoons or drawings and 75 photographs (Tables 1, 2, 3, 4).

Table 1   Media Documents Analysed

Description of Results:	
Number of articles	105
Different authors (13 female, 49 male)	62
Most prolific author (7 articles)	James Christie
Front page articles	13
Column inches	2,509
Cartoons or drawings	7
Photographs	75

Table 2   Content of Photographs Accompanying Articles

38	— of James: 19 alone (including 2 defaced, 2 coaching); 9 with Kennedy (8 same team photo repeated and 1 Memorial Cup winning team)
40	— of Kennedy: 29 alone (including 10 action shots); 9 with James (8 same team photo repeated and 1 Memorial Cup winning team); 2 with wife (or wife and child)
3	— of suspected paedophiles other than James
1	— of other victims than Kennedy
4	— of officials and experts
3	— of media personalities
3	— of players other than Kennedy
2	— of others
Total: 75 Photographs	

Second, we conducted independent analyses using agreed upon criteria[3]. Third, we compared the similarities and differences in our analyses and have used the resultant analyses to "chart the trends in composition and structure..." (Gebner, in Butler and Paisley, 1980: p. 60) to reveal the attitudes of reporters towards homosexuality and sexual abuse in the sport context. National coverage was more extensive than in Ontario or the prairies even though the case was being tried in Winnipeg, Manitoba and involved prairie junior hockey leagues. Three papers, the *Globe and Mail*, *Toronto Star* and *The Winnipeg Free Press* provided 40% of the total coverage.

Table 3   Distribution of Articles in Newspapers, magazines and other sources:

Name:	Number of articles	Number of cartoons	Number of photographs	Number of column inches	% of total coverage
Toronto Star (Ontario)	4	0	1	307	12.2
Globe & Mail (National)	30	1	15	670	26.7
Edmonton Journal (Alberta)	9	0	9	169	
Vancouver Sun (British Columbia)	7	0	1	89	
Calgary Herald (Alberta)	7	0	7	120	
Winnipeg Free Press (Manitoba)	16	3	9	237	9.4
The Ottawa Citizen (Ontario)	7	0	6	1167	
USA Today (International)	3	0	2	44	
Le Journal de Quebec (Quebec)	1	0	3	11	
Le Soleil (Quebec)	1	0	1	22	
Washington Post (International)	2	0	3	67	
The Gazette (Quebec)	4	0	0	66	
New York Times (International)	2	0	3	56	
Winnipeg Sun (Manitoba)	2	0	0	26	
Christian Science Monitor (International)	1	0	1	29	
Alberta Report (Alberta)	1	0	6	88	
Macleans (National)	2	0	8	105	
Canadian Council for Ethics and Sport (National	1	0	0	25	
Manitoban (Manitoba)	2	3	0	40	
Regina Leader Post (Saskatchewan)	1	0	0	15	
CAAWS Action	2	0	0	156	
Total	105	7	75	3509	

Table 4   Distribution of Coverage by Region

	Number of papers / articles	% of coverage
International	4 / 8	7.8%
National	4 / 35	38.1%
Quebec and Atlantic	3 / 6	3.9%
Ontario	2 / 11	18.9%
Prairies	7 / 38	27.7%
British Columbia	<u>1</u> / <u>7</u>	<u>3.5%</u>
TOTALS	21 / 105	100.0%

Results: emerging attitudes towards homophobia and heterosexism

Three main themes focused our attention on homophobia and heterosexism: Sheldon Kennedy as victim, Graham James as a "creep", and the "ugly story" in hockey.

Theme 1: Sheldon Kennedy as victim

There is considerable homophobia and heterosexism evidenced in the media coverage of Kennedy as a victim. Expressions of homophobia were articulated in stories related to Kennedy as victim of a male abuser, a coach, a hockey environment, or public blindness.

a)   Kennedy as victim of a male abuser

First, Kennedy is portrayed as having a *conflicted sexual orientation* and *limited ability to act*. Kennedy felt he may "not be normal": the phrasing used was "I was afraid to come out. I was always afraid I am not normal" (*Ottawa Citizen* and *Washington Post*, 7 January, 1997). The juxtaposition of "come out" and "not normal" is not accidental on the part of the journalists. We also read about the possibility that "some athletes try on their sexuality with coaches, flirting and touching" (*Globe and Mail*, 9 January, 1997). This would suggest that a 32 year old male (James) may not be responsible for the sexual abuse of a 14 year old male (Kennedy) under his direct supervision as a player. During the decade of abuse that ensued, Kennedy reports that "I hated it ... believe me", and that he resisted by running away from James' home in full hockey gear (*Edmonton Journal*,

3 January, 1997) and by convincing James that his behaviour was actually sexually abusive of Kennedy: "I lied. I told James I had been abused before by my grade 7 teacher" *(Ottawa Citizen*, 7 January, 1997).

Second, Kennedy was also portrayed as unable to speak out about sexual abuse because of the macho, gay intolerant environment of hockey. *The Vancouver Sun* reports that Kennedy was "very scared ... not wanting anyone to find out" (7 January, 1997) and that Kennedy "thought he was gay because he was abused by James" (10 January, 1997). The other players seemed to know about the abuse and were continually using gay-related epithets within Kennedy's hearing on the ice *(Ottawa Citizen*, 7 January, 1997).

Given that the abuse Kennedy endured was an open secret among his peers and that they were openly derogatory of his role, it is not surprising that Kennedy expressed considerable self doubt about his own orientation and was frustrated by his inability to act. A particularly vehement article published in the *Alberta Report* concluded that because of the macho culture in hockey, it would be difficult for players to 'come out' or complain. The author then blames organised hockey and an increasingly permissive society for "letting gays wander loose in sport" (20 January, 1997). The *Alberta Report* was not concerned about letting sexual abusers wander loose, just gays.

b)   Kennedy as a victim of his coach

Given that coaches have considerable power over and responsibility for the athletes they coach, portrayals of Kennedy as a victim of his coach show a press confused by the good coach—bad coach scenario. James had an enviable win–loss record as a Junior Hockey coach and had once been awarded the "Coach of the Year". Kennedy is portrayed as "a virtual concubine" *(Washington Post*, 8 January, 1997) of this coach.

The press described a double victimization of Kennedy, first at the hands of James and second, at the hands of a hockey association that believed James was the only coach who could keep a badly behaving Kennedy productive as a player. Kennedy saw himself as an unwilling victim. He stated that James was "in love" with him *(Washington Post)*. Kennedy stated, "It was like we were married or something" *(Le Journal de Quebec*, 7 January, 1997) and "It was like I was his wife or lover ... I believe that Graham truly fell in love with me ... *(Alberta Report*, 20 January, 1997). The sexual abuse of Kennedy was described in detail as sexual acts and attempted sexual acts, and Kennedy claimed he could not fight off his attacker because of James' psychological strength.

The press also discovered that Kennedy had had problems with alcohol abuse and wild behaviour. James positioned himself as the one who could control Kennedy and keep him productive as an athlete. The press reported that the hockey establishment had unwittingly given assent to James' to have close personal contact with Kennedy and in so doing, removed any hope Kennedy had of ending the assaults. There were no reports of Kennedy receiving professional help during his years of abuse by James.

c)   Kennedy as victim of the ice-hockey environment

Kennedy was drafted into Junior ice hockey when he was 14 years old. He moved a thousand miles from his home community and began to realize his dream of becoming a professional hockey player. He was on **the** road to hockey success. How then could more than 300 sexual assaults on Kennedy occur without anyone even being suspicious? Many hockey people had heard rumours about James' unusual behaviour towards Kennedy but maintained "a dome of silence" (Kirby *et al.*, 2000) over the abuse that Kennedy was experiencing.

Also, Kennedy heard the derogatory statements castigating him for being gay and James' favourite. The willingness of Kennedy's peers to stereotype a young male victim as homosexual blinded both players and the management to the glaring questions about the wildly inappropriate behaviour of a coach towards more than one of his players. This is a "blame the victim" approach in hockey.

In media reports, the world of paedophilia collides with the image of a squeaky clean and wholesome world of hockey. When Kennedy first talked with players and management in April, 1996 (*Edmonton Journal*, 6 January, 1997), hockey management did nothing. Later, after James was found guilty, the Canadian Hockey Association disassociated itself from their award-winning coach. Why? Murray Costello, President of the Canadian Hockey Association, said "I'm sure that people of this deviant nature can burrow into an organization and pick a spot for strange ways" (*The Gazette*, 11 January, 1997). The message is that paedophiles are not cultivated from within the ranks of hockey but burrow into the organization to do damage. That hockey structures and functions as fertile ground for the potential development of sexual abusers was not addressed by the hockey establishment.

One atypical article reported that Kennedy's 'problem' in hockey was the result of an increasing permissive society, one where gay tolerance means "men [are] groping and sodomizing young males" (*Alberta Report*, 20 January, 1997). That is, as long as homosexuals run free in sport's macho culture, sexual abuse of young males will continue. Inaction by hockey organizations is seen, at least by the *Alberta Report* writers, as the result of a society increasingly open to treating gays and lesbians as equal and respected members of society.

d)   Kennedy as victim of public blindness

Kennedy is victimized by two things: the inability of the hockey establish-ment and fans to believe the account of sexual abuse even when they are told about it; and the tendency of the public to "sweep the whole thing under the carpet". Despite rumours and innuendo about James, the public hunger for hockey prevented them from asking questions about abuse (*Fifth Estate*, November 1996). It was a shocked, surprised, and stunned public who read about the James' case in the papers. Despite considerable press coverage prior to 1997 on hazing in hockey and sexual harassment and abuse in sport (Kirby and Greaves, 1997), the public seemed to be caught completely unaware.

It is as if "no one did a bloody thing" (*Manitoban*, 29 January, 1997) despite the years of rumours about James and several other hockey coaches and managers. These suspected abusers all rested in the assurance that a "real" hockey player "would never squeal" to the public (*Manitoban*, 29 January, 1997). When Kennedy finally did speak out, he broke ranks with his hockey playing peers, with the coaches and with the hockey management. The public embraced him, but cautiously at first until it became clear in the reports that he had been an unwilling victim, was happily married and was trying to make hockey a better place for future players.

Michelle Landsberg wrote that "our (public) myopia contributes to sex abuse in children" (*Toronto Star,* 20 January, 1997: p. A:14). It is the "glossy armor of respectability that lets sexual predators triumph over and over again". Landsberg concludes that we are in for endless "repeated cycles of revelation and shock".

e)   Transformation of Kennedy from victim to hero

The sexual abuse story finally broke when Kennedy's wife Jana confronted Graham James by telephone, saying:

> " ... you want to get into this right now, Graham? ... He started to backpedal to justify his actions and "I finally said 'Graham, there is no justification. He was a child and you're an adult and you abused your power and trust." (*Edmonton Journal*, 6 January, 1997; Winnipeg Free Press, 7 January 1997)

Most press stories contained some details of the sexual abuse Kennedy had suffered. Since he was happily married and had a supportive wife and child, the public was reassured that the sexual abuse was not just some love relationship between two gay guys, one much younger than the other. Once the sexual orientation of Kennedy was reported as heterosexual, the public and the hockey association warmed to him and, paradoxically, finally seemed anxious to hear every word he had to say.

From 7 January, 1997 onwards, the press portrayed Kennedy as a paragon of virtue, one who was courageous enough to break the long standing pattern of secrecy around the naming of sexual abuse victims. (*Calgary Press*, 29 October, 1996). In December, 1997, Kennedy was named 'newsmaker of the year'. A year and one-half later the press were hovering over the second, as yet unidentified victim for him to release his story.

Theme 2: Graham James as a "creep"

a)   James portrayed as having a past record, though relatively hidden one

The accounts, drawn from a series of newspapers portray James as a man with a long history of problematic behaviour. It reported that in 1984, a group of players had "demanded that James be fired because his sexuality was having a negative effect on his coaching" (*Globe and Mail*, 14 January, 1997: A1). In 1992, James was charged with assault during a hockey game when he retaliated against a fan. In early 1994, James dropped all his clothes except for his shorts while he was coaching a game (Mitchell, *Globe and Mail* J14). The allegations of misconduct attracted little public attention (*Toronto Star*, 23 October, 1996).

There are numerous indications that James had problems establishing appropriate boundaries between himself and his players, and had displayed quite inappropriate behaviours with hockey fans and referees. Note that the 1984 action by players asking for James' resignation is reported as a problem with James' sexual orientation rather than as sexually abusive behaviour. This was during the period when he was abusing Kennedy every Tuesday and Thursday evening during the hockey season. The players' willingness to interpret the problem as sexual orientation illustrates that homophobia is perhaps stronger than players' willingness to accept the possibility of sexual abuse in their ranks. James is portrayed as:

...   calculating, that he had already selected his next engaged victim by establishing an RRSP out of his own money for the player and taking him on out-of-town trips (*The Ottawa Citizen*, 11 January, 1997);

...   perverse, that James was on the dark side of hockey and apparently "routinely paid players to have sex with women while he watched ...." (Robinson, 1998; McCarten, *The Vancouver Sun*, 13 January, 1997);

... being in love with a young boy (*Alberta Report*, 20 January, 1997); and

... being a controller where his "infatuation with his new companion got a little out of control and was at times 'blatant and disturbing' ... it became overt!" (*Alberta Report*, 20 January, 1997).

His sexual predation is directly intertwined with his sexual orientation and there is no effort on the part of the press to separate abusive behaviour and sexuality. If one reads only the *Alberta Report* account, one would be led to believe that James was an homosexual infatuated with young players rather than a paedophile. This sensationalist coverage of James' orientation is despite a wealth of research which indicates that paedophiles choose vulnerable victims because they can groom them and establish a pattern of escalating abuse with relative impunity.

b)   James and other abusers

The press went to some lengths to compare James' behaviour to that of other abusers. On 6 January, 1997, a single comparison was made between abusers in sport and those in the church and the military. Given the high profile national and international cases in the press at the time, it is surprising that this only appeared once.

Homophobia was most evidentbin the *Alberta Report* article (20 January, 1997: p.31). This particularly vicious article contains subtitles such as "Depravity in the Dressing Room", "Hockey Pays for Price of Gay Tolerance" and "The Ugly Truth about Predatory Homosexual Coaches Finally Comes Out". According to Sillars (*The Alberta Report*, 20 January,1997), sodomy is in sport's macho culture. He believed that homosexuals run free because they are finding increased acceptance in sport. The article's stance is supported by Landolt, lawyer and president of REAL Women (a right wing; anti-equality group), Hannon (an advocate for "intergenerational sex) and Cherry (a producer of a series of videos featuring hockey violence — "Rock'em Sock'em Hockey"). Inflammatory phrases about sexual abuse by James were used: "sordid scandal, predatory homosexual", "the triumph of the gay agenda", and "limp-wristed players or coaches". These appeal to the worst of stereotypes about gay men, that they live sordid lives, groping and sodomizing boys. No distinction is made between James, the abuser, and Kennedy, the victim when a phrase like "limp wristed players or coaches" is used.

Only one article in *The Winnipeg Free Press* actually followed up on issues raised by the *Alberta Report*. Using a backdrop of other cases of sexual abuse in sport and the 1984 Badgley Report on "Sexual Offences Against Children", *The Winnipeg Free Press* journalist, Galloway, writes about "society's darker and dirtier corners" and of the misconduct of gay coaches. She challenges the connection between sexual abuse and homosexuality by suggesting that paedophiles don't care about the sex of the child they assault.

c)   James the S.O.B.

The press seemed to have no difficulty in maligning Graham James. After he pleaded guilty he was variously portrayed as "sick", a "creep", a "demon", a paedophile, a sexual predator and as the doer of heinous deeds. He was described as being on the bottom of the totem pole, an S.O.B., one no one could now trust. Reporters described James' sexual control over his victims, and, in the case of Sheldon Kennedy, that James had "stolen Kennedy's trust". Some saw James as a gay man who actually "broke down and confessed he was gay", as if homosexuals must "confess" to their sexual orientation. All in all, the coverage of James was an uncritical integration of his sexual predation and his presumed sexual orientation. When Dan Cherry (a hockey commentator and critic) suggested, "I'd have drawn and quartered the S.O.B.", it appeared that many had conveniently forgotten how enthusiastically they had written about James as a winning coach and 'Coach of the Year' just a short time earlier.

d)   James' defence

Very little attention is paid to the actual words of Graham James. Normally in sexual abuse cases, there are numerous references to accounts by the abusers but little or none by the victim. Since Kennedy went public, much of what we "know" about James comes from Kennedy or from the press.

There seems to be some confusion about what James thought. The press coverage suggests that James was "in love with a young player" (Globe and Mail, 14 January, 1997) rather than a paedophile:

> I guess I just wished it were acceptable. Maybe I thought I was living in Ancient Greece or something like that ... I cared about people. I only crossed the line a couple of times." (Edmonton Journal, 8 January, 1997)

Theme 3: Media descriptions of the horror of sexual abuse

In addition to the media narratives about Kennedy and James, there was also evidence in the print media about the impact that this sexual abuse would have on the "sacred" and "hallowed ground" of ice hockey (De Palma, *The New York Times*, 16 January, 1997: p. A1).

> It is scaring people ... There is a malignancy. We are a very insecure
> country. Our security in the last 40 to 50 years has been based on
> our perceived — or misperceived — hockey supremacy. We just
> believe in this thing. It's a fantasy world. A lot of people have put
> their hands over their eyes and ears ... And now we see the sordid
> underbelly." (Roy Macgregor, quoted in Lapointe, *The New York
> Times*, 23 February, 1997: p. 3)

In the first report we collected regarding the news of Graham James's
sexual charges (*The Toronto Star*, 23 October, 1996) we have the first
glimpse of the "shock wave" this abuse will have on hockey. The Canadian
Hockey Association President, however, assures the writer (and the
audience) that although "it will be embarrassing for us all ... I do not think
it will have profound repercussions," nor will the whole game of hockey be
destroyed by "one bad apple" (p. C1). By 3 January, 1997, when James
pleaded guilty, the "embarrassing situation" had turned into "a very sad day
for us" in which the "shock of these events to the hockey community is
devastating" (Mofina, *The Calgary Herald*, 3 January, 1997). As the story
continued over the next three days, the statements appearing in the media
(issued from the hockey industry) framed the sexual abuse as "a tragedy,"
"a frightening situation," "hard to believe," and a "dark day for hockey"
(Campbell, *The Globe and Mail*, 4 January, 1997).

Although child sexual abuse is a problem at large in Canadian society
(*Macleans*, 10 February, 1997), ice hockey became a powerful symbol to
draw Canada's attention to it.

> For Canadians to accept that hockey — long called "Canada's true
> religion" is vulnerable — is hard. This is our essence, everything
> that we are, so when it happens to our teams, it happens to us ...
> Canadians have a very sentimental view of hockey ... Canadians
> have such faith in hockey that we believed it had a purity that cast
> a spell over everything and everyone .... (Roy Macgregor quoted in
> Clayton, *The Christian Science Monitor*, 16 January, 1997: p. 9)

Yet part of the reason why the story was framed as such a "nightmare" was
because the "sordid world of paedophilia collided with Canada's most
wholesome symbol" (Wong, *The Globe and Mail*, 13 January, 1997: p. A1).
In addition to Kennedy being robbed of his innocence in this "sordid" affair,
the media narrative communicated to the reader that the affair "robbed the
whole hockey loving nation of innocence" (Christie and Langford, *The Globe
and Mail*, 1 February, 1997). In this way the media framed James as

victimizing an entire sport. He and his ugly deeds were constructed in opposition to the wholesomeness of hockey, a deeply Canadian ritual. It is interesting to note, however, that in *The Globe and Mail* article written by Wong (13 January, 1997) we were presented with information that contradicts this innocent imagery of hockey. The subculture of junior hockey, we learn, has its own rituals which include the hazing of rookie (first year) players. Wong tells us that " ... last year and the year before teammates stripped first-year players, tied their clothes in knots and made them sit for hours, naked, in the toilet compartment of the bus ... " (p. A2). This is the only mention of the less than wholesome side of junior hockey (outside of other sexual abuse cases) contained in the articles[4] .By ignoring this aspect of hockey, its "sordid underbelly" was constructed as solely the result of Graham James and "his ilk," James, and like deviants, could be distanced from the reader. Many of the readers may in fact have understood these less than pure images of hockey but may have explained them away as 'boys will be boys' and/or 'that's hockey.'

The media narratives also contained reactions from those involved in hockey. These reactions conveyed the utter shock that those individuals were feeling regarding the news of this case. One coach was reported as saying that "it made me sick to my stomach," while another stated that "for something like this to happen in hockey makes it worse" (Schneider and Alexander, *The Washington Post*, 8 January, 1997: p. D4). The Canadian Hockey League president was quoted as saying, "I don't think junior hockey has ever had a more trying week. it's been sickening. There are not many things worse. It tears away the innocence we thought was in our sport." (p. A1). One hockey executive went so far as to call the scandal a "scab" that might never heal (DePalma, *The New York Times*, 16 January, 1997).

Other language that was used depicted the abuse story as "a harrowing tale, "a horrible story" (*Maclean's*,, 20 January, 1997: p. 54), and an "abusive nightmare" (Campbell, *The Globe and Mail*, May 19, 1997) which was "horrifying to people" (Sillars, *The Alberta Report*, 20 January,1997).

This discourse appeared to capture Canadians' visceral reaction to this sexual abuse case. All the words and metaphors that we associate with 'unpleasantness' were prevalent. The intent of the writers appears to be to link these shocked reactions alongside the same-sex nature of the abuse to compound the feelings of horror.

We learn through the media that part of the 'ugliness' of this abuse was not just that it 'tarnished' hockey. First, it was horrific because the power entrusted to James was abused turning the dreams of young athletes into nightmares.

> Sheldon Kennedy had a dream. Graham James took it, crumpled it up and gave Kennedy something in place of that dream: a nightmare. (Herstein, *The Manitoban*, 28 January,1997: p. 9)

In this case James was framed as the betrayer whose part in the "sickly tale of shattered faith" (Maki, *The Vancouver Sun*, 9 January, 1997: p. F2) was so much more despised because he was once so revered, he had been put on a pedestal as a coach. Christie, *The Globe and Mail* states:

> In the case of junior hockey, a coach has the power to crush a young player's life long dream, just when it's within reach. (January 11, 1997)

The narratives that framed the sexual abuse as a "power that turned sour" (Bray, *The Montreal Gazette*, 11 January, 1997: p. A16) took the emphasis off the sexual nature of the abuse and placed it on the abuse of power. This discourse had the potential to make the public recognize the propensity to abuse power amongst themselves and so see themselves as potential sexual abusers. Framing the case as an abuse of power contradicted the press' construction of difference.

It was a 'horrifying story' because there was a suspicion throughout the story's run that the abuse may have been ignored. We learn that there was a "crisis of conscience as Swift Current sifts through its collective memory to try to figure out who knew what, and when about the sexual assaults ..." (Mitchell, *The Globe and Mail*, 14 January, 1997: p. A6). Allegations were directed towards managers and administrators in the Western Hockey League (WHL) who were accused of not investigating 'rumors' about James'. It was believed that:

> Graham James ... felt he could prey on players with impunity... "if you're Graham James and you were looking at this league and saw that this [Mr. Shaw's abuse of players] is not a problem, no wonder he felt he could prey on them." (Houston Campbell, *The Globe and Mail*, 9 January, 1997: p. A1).

The place of hockey in Canadian society was also subject to accusations because of its mythology. The fact that it is "the gateway to heroism, manhood and millions of dollars" (Christie, *The Globe and Mail*, 8 January, 1997) was blamed for exposing vulnerable youths to sexual predators; the "system allows them to be treated like pieces of meat and victimized to keep alive a dream of playing professional hockey" (Christie, *The Globe and Mail*, 11 January, 1997: pp. A1, A22). Landsberg of *The Toronto Star* commented:

Another parent who is also a coach swore that 'hockey is the most important institution in Canada. Get a grip, people. Hockey is a game, a big business, a pastime, a way to sell beer — it's not sacred and it is not equivalent to the Canadian identity. Scores of Canadian boys have been and will be molested by coaches because adults think hockey is so damned important that the whole structure of it is unquestionable. (18 January, 1997: p. A14)

The Alberta Report extends its blame beyond hockey. We read, "Homosexual predation affects women's sports too." Links are made from gay males, who are sexual predators, to lesbians. Statements suggested that "females are more likely to abuse power in a sports relationship"; that the "problem of abuse is acute in sports which have a high percentage of lesbians" (they list women's hockey, softball and golf); and that the abuse of power for sexual purposes in women's sport is almost always homosexual" (p. 33). These statements lead readers to the conclusion that "lesbian coaches and senior players [are] attempting to recruit newcomers to a gay lifestyle." The substantiating evidence is the opinion of a female sports psychologist. Readers of *The Alberta Report* were "told to brace themselves for more deviants to pop up behind the benches of young hockey players" and that "to these homosexual predators, the dressing rooms of pubescent boys are no longer off limits" (p. 31). The choice of language in this article is intentional, and meant to stir up hatred and moral panic about gays and lesbians in sport.

Discussion: moral panic, discourse of sexuality, and Davis's ideal subject position

In the print media's descriptions of the horror of abuse the language was repeatedly used to illustrate the utter 'ugliness' of this sexual abuse case. Through their stories (using their own narratives and the responses of others) the media communicated clearly a sense of disgust and shock at the news of sexual abuse in hockey.

Through the narratives that (re)constructed, James as "creep," Kennedy as "victim," the graphic descriptions of the abuse and its horror, the whole community inside and outside hockey we were sensitized to the risks of sexual abuse in sport. These stories framed the abuse as something that victimized all of Canada (*The Calgary Herald*, 3 January 1997), and warned the public that nothing could be taken for granted in ice hockey again (Editorial, *The Winnipeg Free Press*, 8 January, 1997).

Although these stories were a catalyst for exposing sexual abuse we would suggest that the language used to describe this "harrowing tale" also succeeded in generating a "moral panic" (Donnelly and Sparkes, 1997) among readers who had an investment in the world of hockey and sports. From *Maclean's* (10 February, 1997) we learn that "plenty of parents across Canada are experiencing anxieties ... Graham James is largely responsible for that" (p. 42), and that "Canadian Hockey ... has been flooded with calls from parents concerned there might be more sexual predators in minor hockey's coaching ranks" (Bray, *The Ottawa Citizen*, 11 January, 1997).

In a recent study (Kirby and Greaves, 1997) it was reported that male athlete's were particularly fearful of their children being sexually abused if and when they had them. This fear appears to extend to parents in general, given the storylines in the articles. It is not difficult to suggest that telling the readers that there are 15,000 opportunities to have good or bad coaches in hockey contributes towards creating moral indignation and panic among various readers. In addition, the stories were often framed around narratives that described James as a (homo)sexual predator, Kennedy as a vulnerable farm-boy, and graphic descriptions of sexual acts.

Each reader is influenced by his/her particular socio-historical location. Thus decoding and reconstructing meaning may take place from hegemonic, negotiated (those who may accept the text's assumptions with some adaptations) or oppositional positions (Hall, 1984). However, given the links between sports, hegemonic masculinity and 'compulsory heterosexuality' (Davis, 1993) we would suggest that the encoded messages produced, subtle and sometimes blatant, heterosexist and homophobic discourses. The fact that the majority of boys and men's sports are coached by men, and that the abusive situations between players and coach have been, and may be again, 'same-sex' abuse, compounds the fears and anxieties of a heteronormative sports society, and encourages the reading of these stories in a particular way.

> ... though events will not be systematically encoded in a single way, they will tend, systematically, to draw on a very limited repertoire: and that repertoire ... will have the overall tendency of making things "mean" within the sphere of dominant ideology. (Hall, 1977 in Birrell and Cole, 1994: p. 379).

If producers of media text are encouraging a preferred reading then they will be reliant on an audience who will decode the reading from a dominant or hegemonic position (those who do not question the text's assumptions) rather than those who will decode the reading from an oppositional position (those who question the text's assumptions) (Hall, 1984). In other words the producers may be delivering to an "ideal subject position":

> An ideal subject position is the type of reader that the text beckons through its structure and content. Examining the textual structure and content for suggestions of the preferred identities and perspectives of potential readers or viewers reveals the ideal subject position. The ideal subject position suggests the identities and perspectives that the producers assume to prevail among their readership and/or those whom the producers desire to read the texts .... (Davis, 1993: pp. 169–170)

In the media's stories about the Sheldon Kennedy/Graham James sexual abuse case we suggest that the discourses used called forth a preferred reading of the texts, a reading in which difference and opposition was constructed through the framing of James's and Kennedy's sexual identities.

a)   Heterosexual framing

Davis (1993) tells us that this "ideal subject position" in much of Western media "calls forth Western, white, heterosexual, and men viewers" (p. 170). We suggested that the reading of the Kennedy/James sexual abuse story certainly calls forth heterosexual male readers. Kennedy is presented by the media and through his own declarations, as heterosexual.

We believe the media's intent was to 'answer' the confusions and contradictions that may have existed surrounding the association between hockey and masculinity and these masculine hockey boys being subjected to (homo)sexual abuse. This theme was confirmed when we read that "the victims, especially boys in the macho environment of sports, feel ashamed for not being able to take care of themselves" (*Maclean's*, 20 January, 1997: p. 55). Donnelly and Sparks (1997) state:

> There is ... shame associated with homosexual abuse in the world of macho sports; it is easy to feel that one's peers would believe that one should have been able to prevent it, and that if one did not, it must have been consensual. (p. 202)

We also learn that "Jana (Kennedy's wife) has been at her husband's side, supporting him since he decided last spring to come forward with the allegations against James" (*The Ottawa Citizen*, 7 January, 1997: p. C8). The depiction of his wife supporting him and being critical in his decision and ability to come forward about the abuse confirms traditional (hetero)sexist standards and conforms to dominant ideologies of gender relations. Furthermore, the depictions of Kennedy as a capable, reproducing, heterosexual male confirmed his heterosexual status.

b)   Framing the heterosexual family

"As a parent this story is one of your worst nightmares." (Korn-heiser, *The Washington Post*, 8January, 1997: p. D4)

The fact that the reports often appeared as "news" stories as well as "sports" stories suggest that this story about abuse in ice hockey transcended sports. We suggest that the "ideal subject position" be extended beyond the heterosexual male reader in this case. Another "ideal subject position" elicited was that of heterosexual parent(s). The discourse used in many of the reports summoned up imagery of the vulnerability of young children in sport (particularly boys in hockey) to sexual predators.

It's a sensitive subject because it's such a macho sport ... " ... "It's scary as a parent. He's a country boy ... We're kind of naive when it comes to some of these things. And you don't know what goes on. They're so close-mouthed about what goes on in the dressing room." (Two mothers quoted in Wong, *The Globe and Mail*, 13 January, 1997: p. A2)

"Junior hockey coaches have so much control over the future of their young players that they can do almost anything they please" (Taylor, *The Winnipeg Free Press*, 7 January, 1997). In addition, headlines and stories urged parents to be more vigilant in their children's sports careers, they are called on to be "the first line of defence against abuse" (*The Ottawa Citizen*, 11 January, 1997: p. G2) and to "provide ... armor to protect their loved ones" (Engler, *The Vancouver Sun*, 9 January, 1997: p. F1). These calls for protection serve to call forth the "ideal subject position" of parent(s), most probably heterosexual parent(s).

Text and photographs also showed Kennedy's (hetero)sexual status as father, husband, and family man. Kennedy is pictured with his wife Jana and daughter Ryan in an article honouring his courage in talking about his experiences of abuse (*The Globe and Mail*, 1 February, 1997). Placing Kennedy's heterosexual family along with text in which the media report that his goal was to; "picnic with his wife and not think of the years James stole from him" (USA Today, 7 January, 1997: p. 3B), to "hang out with [his] wife and daughter (*The Globe and Mail*, 9 January, 1997: p. A13), and "to be the best father and husband [he] could be (*The Globe and Mail*, 1 February, 1997: p. A27) serves not only to confirm his heterosexual status but summoned the audience to recognize itself in this heterosexual family unit.

c)   Homosexual framing, the positioning of 'The Other'

James' sexual behaviour and the sexual acts linked to his sexual orientation were encoded and read as deviant, as distinct from (hetero)sexual normative standards. Kimmel (1994) states:

> Within the dominant culture, the masculinity that defines white, middle class, early middle-aged, heterosexual men is the masculinity that sets the standards for other men, against which other men are measured and, more often than not, found wanting. (pp. 124–125)

The framing of James as the 'weak' homosexual ("[he] broke down") defines his masculinity in opposition to his players, because "We equate manhood with being strong, successful, capable, reliable, in control" (Kimmel, 1994: p. 125).

In the media stories James is certainly not framed as a "real" (hetero) man, he is "found wanting" in many areas of manhood. Further, the language used to describe the sexual acts themselves juxtaposed with the framing of James as a homosexual and Kennedy as a heterosexual created a reading of homosexual sex as deviant.

One could argue that the media were merely reporting James as homosexual because he himself identified as such. In fact in some texts not only do we read that James identifies as homosexual but he positions Kennedy in opposition to his own reported sexual orientation. It may be suggested that by positioning himself as a homosexual, who was merely "in love" with his two players, James was defining himself in opposition to the paedophile 'other', which is even more negatively viewed than a homosexual identity. However, by positioning Kennedy as heterosexual, James will always be read as homosexual abuser and deviant.

Finally, the press' framing of homosexual extended beyond the primary story of the Kennedy/James sexual abuse case and included other stories of abuse that had homosexual connections. Thus, consciously or subconsciously, the heterosexual reader's fear that sports are rife with abusive coaches, who through the framing of the stories were often positioned as homosexual, is solidified.

Conclusion — constructing oppositions

However, there was evidence of alternative and/or counter hegemonic responses to the linking of homosexuality to paedophilia. Campbell (*The*

Globe and Mail, 4 January, 1997) writes, "Several people have said there were rumors that James was gay, as if that has anything to do with it, as if being homosexual automatically means individuals cannot control themselves" (p. A22). Similarly, Engler (*The Vancouver Sun*, 9 January, 1997) reports that "many parents resist what might seem reasonable and important information to some, like making clear the difference between homosexuality and paedophilia" (p. F2). We acknowledge that it was not a simple case of heterosexist moralizing and homophobic bias among the journalists who wrote the stories (although in some cases homophobia was blatant). Various constraints placed on the media work to encode some meaning and not others. These constraints occur at many levels; work routines, professional ideologies, and social, cultural and commercial forces (Cantelon and Gruneau, 1988; Jhally, 1989) bringing "pressures to bear on the sports journalist" (Wenner, 1989: p. 43). Due to the primacy of heterosexual discourse in our society (Fuss, 1991; Namaste, 1994) these stories may inevitably be framed within a 'homophile context.' Thus the moral high ground is constructed from the "ideal subject position" of heterosexual.

The fact that the homosexuality of James and the heterosexuality of Kennedy were framed at all in these stories seriously taints the media's coverage of the sexual abuse case. To position homosexuality at all with paedophilia and abuse suggests a preferred reading that positions the homosexual as the villain, the 'other', and the heterosexual as the victim thus "incite(ing) the posses of hearsay" (Babington, 1993: p. 495; also Kelly *et al.*, 1995). Despite the disclaimers of the links between homosexuality and paedophilia, or the failure to mention it at all[5], the representation of James as the (homo)sexual predator serves to reinforce conscious and subconscious stereotypes based on existing heteronormative discourses of power. In the thirty-four articles that either explicitly framed James as homosexual and/or Kennedy as heterosexual there were relatively few, five in all, that attempted to articulate the assumptions and stereotypes about homosexuals/heterosexuals and paedophilia inherent in these discourses. Framing the two subjects, and other role players (parents, Brian Shaw, friends of James) in this "swirling morass" of sexual abuse in the stories as either heterosexual or homosexual suggests the likelihood of a heteronormative interpretation of the texts.

The "outlaws" who abuse power in sport must be exposed. As Babington (1993) states:

> ... when it comes to the welfare of children, society is vigilant; every
> threat of sexual violence must be neutralized, utterly. We hear, see,
> and read about what is told, shown, and written in the language of

the media. From it we formulate the language of public outcry against those monstrous outlaws who scheme to strip away the very innocence and the very lives of our youngsters. (p. 495)

When those "monstrous outlaws" are framed or positioned as (homo)sexual deviants it only serves to confirm the boundaries of heterosexual and homosexual society, "shore(ing) up the ontological boundaries of heterosexuality" (Fuss, 1991: p. 2) while protecting its rightness and righteousness (Pharr, 1988).

As part of their delivery to the "ideal subject position" the media (and journalists writing the stories) acted as moral arbitrators about sexual abuse in sports. They did act to raise the consciousness surrounding abuse in ice hockey and the abuse of power by 'abusive' coaches, but from our oppositional reading they appeared to "stake out some moral high ground, [in] identifying clear evil" (Babington, 1993: p. 492), unfortunately this evil was sometimes framed as the homosexual 'other.'

Currently the existence of sexual abuse and harassment in sports such as hockey is becoming increasingly difficult to deny. It is essential that stories like the Kennedy/James case be heard so that the "dome of silence" (Kirby *et al.*, 1998) over sexual abuse and harassment in sport does not continue. Given the information presented in this paper, however, we believe that there is a responsibility to report these stories in a way that does not create moral panic among the readers. Ormsby states that, despite the "gruesome exceptions":

No one wants to curb the joy of a young one's athletic participation because well-meaning adults have unwittingly created monstrous bogeymen in their minds. Children should not be paralyzed by fear and should be reassured that most grown-ups involved in sport are honest, sincere and would never dream of hurting someone. (*The Toronto Star,* 4 May, 1997: pp. E5–E6)

Finally, it is important that in writing and reading these stories a variety of approaches are to reach diverse audiences. Although Kennedy's heterosexuality and James' homosexuality were constantly foregrounded there were no expert voices around the issue of sport and sexuality included in the print media's commentary on the case. Given the absence of these voices it was, and is, necessary to continue to analyze the media as "material contexts within which heterosexuality is constructed" (Messner, 1996: p. 231). Such an approach encourages alternative and counter hegemonic readings and better informs the audience to think critically about the issues of sexual abuse in sport.

Notes

1 Sexual abuse is a difficult term to define. As Kirby and Brackenridge (1998) indicate:

> "...a plethora of terms for sexual abuse exist, among them: sexual harassment, chilly climate (Lenskyj, (1994), sexual assault, sexual predation (CCES), sexual exploitation and grooming (Gonsiorek, 1995; Brackenridge, 1996), child pornography, child prostitution and trafficking (Kelly *et al.*, 1995) and distinctive forms of abuse which occur within family (incest, child abuse, child sexual abuse, wife abuse and family violence)."

Terms common in media articles about adult sexual perpetrators and children label the abusers paedophiles, pederasts, child sexual assaulters, and more recently, hebophiles. All terms have specific meanings but in Canada, the term "paedophile" is used in sexual abuse cases to generally refer to adults who sexual abuse children under 18 years of age.

2 In the case of Messner and Solomon (1994), the news frames were from stories on Sugar Ray Leonard's drug and wife abuse.

3 These criteria include location (news/sports/other, page number, right/left, top/bottom); size (column inches); general focus; specific content related to manifest/latent homophobia; and author/publication.

4 That this information (or previous stories on the rituals of hazings broadcast by the Canadian Broadcasting Corporation on the Fifth Estate program, October 1996) was not unpacked in other media narratives may be important.

5 In the *Alberta Report,* Sillar's comments on the media's studious avoidance of James' homosexuality. First, this is untrue. Second, it is important to look at the significance of framing Kennedy as heterosexual as much as the framing of James as homosexual.

References

Babington, D. (1993) 'Sexual outlaws and the posses of hearsay', *Queen's Quarterly*, 100: pp. 491–503.

Birrell, S. (1988) 'Discourses on the gender/sport relationship: From women in sport to gender relations', in K. B. Pandolf (ed), *Exercise and Sport Science Reviews*. New York: MacMillan, pp. 459–502.

Birrell, S. and Cole, C. (1994) 'Double fault: Renee Richards and the construction and naturalization of difference', in S. Birrell and C. Cole (eds), *Women, sport, and culture*. Champaign, IL: Human Kinetics, pp. 373–397.

Boutilier, M., and San Giovanni, L. (1983) *The sporting women*. Champaign, IL: Human Kinetics.

Brackenridge, C. H. (1996) *Healthy sport for healthy girls? The role of parents in preventing sexual abuse in sport*. Paper presented at the Pre-Olympic Scientific Congress, Dallas, USA.

Bryson, L. (1987) 'Sport and the maintenance of masculine hegemony', *Women's Studies International Forum* 10: pp. 349–360.

Butler, M., and Paisley, W. (1980) *Women and the mass media: sourcebook for research and action*. New York: Human Sciences Press, Inc.

Cantelon, H. and Gruneau, R. (1988) 'The production of sport for television', in J. Harvey and H. Cantelon (eds), *Not just a game: essays in Canadian sport sociology*. Ottawa, ON: University of Ottawa Press, pp. 195–211.

Carlisle-Duncan, M. (1990) 'Sports photographs and sexual difference: Images of women and men in the 1984 and 1988 Olympic Games', *Sociology of Sport Journal*, 7 (1): pp. 22–43.

Connell, R. W. (1990) 'An iron man: The body and some contradictions of hegemonic mas culinity', in M. Messner and D. Sabo (eds), *Sport, men and the gender order: Critical feminist perspectives*. Champaign, IL: Human Kinetics, pp. 83–95.

Crosset, T. (1990) 'Masculinity, sexuality, and the development of early modern sport', in M. Messner and D. Sabo (eds), *Sport, men and the gender order: Critical feminist perspectives*. Champaign, IL: Human Kinetics.

Davis, L. (1993) 'Critical analysis of the popular media and the concept of the ideal subject position: Sport Illustrated as a case study', *Quest*, 45, 165–181.

Donnelly, P., and Sparkes, R. (1997) 'Moral panic. Child sexual abuse in sport', in P. Donnelly (ed), *Taking sport seriously: Social issues in Canadian sport*. Toronto: Thompson Educational Publishing.

Dunning, E. (1994) Sport as a male preserve: Notes on the social sources of masculine identity and its transformations', in S. Birrell and C. Cole. (eds), *Women, sport, and culture*. Champaign, IL: Human Kinetics, pp. 163–179.

Fuss, D. (1991) 'Inside/Out', in D. Fuss (ed), *Inside/Out: Lesbian theories, gay theories*. New York: Routledge.

Gonsiorek, J. C. (1995) *Breach of trust: Sexual exploitation by health care professional and clergy*. London: Sage.

Gruneau, R., and Whitson, D. (1993) *Hockey night in Canada: Sport, identities and cultural politics*. Toronto: Garamond Press.

Hall, A. (1988) 'The discourse of gender and sport: From femininity to feminism', *Sociology of Sport Journal* 5: pp. 330–340.

Hall, S. (1984) 'Encoding/decoding', in S. Hall, D. Hobson, A. Lowe, and P. Willis (eds), *Culture, media, language: Working papers in Cultural Studies, 1972–1979*. London: Hutchinson and University of Birmingham, Centre for Contemporary Cultural Studies, pp. 128–138.

Jackson, S. (1994) 'Gretzky, crisis, and Canadian identity in 1988: Re-articulating the Americanization of culture debate', *Sociology of Sport Journal*, 11: pp. 428–446.

Jhally, S. (1989) 'Cultural studies and the sports/media complex', in L. Wenner (ed), *Media, sports, and society*. Newbury Park, CA. Sage, pp. 70–93.

Kane, M. J. (1995) 'Resistance/transformation of the oppositional binary: Exposing sport as a continuum', *Journal of Sport and Social Issues* 19: pp. 191–218.

Kelly, L., Wingfield, R., Burton, S., and Regan, L. (1995) *Splintered lives: Sexual exploitation of children in the context of children's rights*. Essex: Barnardo's.

Kidd, B. (1990) 'The men's cultural centre: Sports and the dynamic of women's oppression/men's repression', in M. Messner and D. Sabo (eds), *Sport, men and the gender order: Critical feminist perspectives*. Champaign, IL: Human Kinetics, pp. 31–43.

King, S. (1993) 'The politics of the body and the body politic: Magic Johnson and the ideology of AIDS', *Sociology of Sport Journal*, 10: pp. 270–285.

Kirby, S. L., and Brackenridge, C. H. (1998) *Coming to terms with sexual abuse*. Unpublished manuscript.

Kirby, S. L., and Greaves, L. (1997) 'Le jeu interdit: La harcelement sexualle dans le sport', *Researches Feministe* 10 (1).

Kirby, S. L., Greaves, L., and Hankinvsky, O. (2000) *The dome of silence: Sexual harassment and abuse in sport*. Halifax: Fernwood.

Klein, A. (1990) 'Little big man: Hustling, gender narcissism, and body building subculture', in M. Messner and D. Sabo (eds), *Sport, men and the gender order: Critical feminist perspectives*. Champaign, IL: Human Kinetics, pp. 127–139.

Lenskyj, H. (1987) 'Female sexuality and women's sport', *Women's Studies International Forum* 10, pp. 381–386.

Lenskyj, H. (1991) 'Combating homophobia in sport and physical education', *Sociology of Sport Journal*, 8 (1): pp. 61–69.

Lenskyj, H. (1994) *Women, sport and physical activity: Selected research themes*. Ottawa, ON: Sport Canada.

Lowes, M. D. (1997) 'Sports pages: A case study in the manufacture of sport news for the daily press', *Sociology of Sport Journal*, 14: pp. 143–159.

MacNeill, M. (1988) 'Active women, media representations and ideology', in J. Harvey and H. Cantelon (eds), *Not just a game: essays in Canadian sport sociology*. Ottawa, ON: University of Ottawa Press, pp. 177–193.

Messner, M. (1996) 'Studying up on sex', *Sociology of Sport Journal*, 13: pp. 221–237.

Messner, M., and Sabo, D. (1994) *Sex, violence and power in sports: Rethinking masculinity*. Freedom, CA: The Crossing Press.

Messner, M., and Solomon, W. (1994) 'Sin and redemption: The Sugar Ray Leonard wife-abuse story', in M. Messner and D. Sabo (eds), *Sex, violence and power in sports: Rethinking masculinity*. Freedom, CA: The Crossing Press.

Namaste, K. (1994) 'The politics of inside/out: Queer theory, poststructuralism, and a sociological approach to sexuality', *Sociological Theory*, 12 (2): pp. 220–231.

Peelo, M., and Soothill, K. (1994) 'Personal power and public control: Sex crimes and problem pages', *The Howard Journal*, 33 (1): pp. 10–24.

Pharr, S. (1988) *Homophobia: A weapon of sexism*. Little Rock, AR: Chardon Press.

Pronger, B. (1990) *The arena of masculinity: Sports, homosexuality, and the meaning of sex*. New York: St. Martin's Press.

Robinson, L. (1998) *Crossing the line: Sexual assault in Canada's national sport*. Toronto: McClelland and Stewart.

Rowe, D. (1994) 'Accommodating bodies: Celebrity, sexuality, and "tragic Magic"', *Journal of Sport and Social Issues*, 18 (1): pp. 6–26.

Therberge, N. (1989) 'A feminist analysis of responses to sports violence: Media coverage of the 1987 world junior hockey championship', *Sociology of Sport Journal*, 6: pp. 247–256.

Theberge, N., and Cronk, A. (1986) Work routines in newspaper sports departments and the coverage of women's sports', *Sociology of Sport Journal*, 3: pp. 195–203.

Wenner, L. (1989) 'Media, sports, and society: The research agenda', in L. Wenner, (ed), *Media, sports, and society*. Newbury Park, CA. Sage, pp. 13–48.

Wheatley, E. (1994) 'Subcultural subversions: Comparing discourses on sexuality in men's and women's rugby songs', in S. Birrell and C. Cole. (eds), *Women, sport, and culture*. Champaign, IL: Human Kinetics, pp. 373–397.

White, P. G., and Vagi, A. B. (1990) 'Rugby in the 19th-century British boarding-school system: a feminist psychoanalytic perspective', in M. Messner and D. Sabo (eds), *Sport, men and the gender order: Critical feminist perspectives*. Champaign, IL: Human Kinetics, pp. 67–78.

Willis, P. (1982) 'Women in sport in ideology', in J. Hargreaves (ed), *Sport, culture and ideology*. London: Routledge and Kegan Paul, pp. 117–135.

Crossing Borders:
Lesbian Physical Education Students and the Struggles for Sexual Spaces

Gill Clarke

Research and Graduate School of Education,
University of Southampton (UK)

Introduction

Theorising the experiences of lesbian students is no easy task, thus, in seeking to make sense of their sexual subjectivities and material realities I am committed to the application of lesbian feminism[1], whilst also drawing on tenets from postmodernism and poststructuralism (see Clarke, 1998b). Such a positioning recognises that there are many ways of knowing and that there is no longer the certainty of grand and fixed narratives of 'absolutes'. Rather, it is acknowledged that all knowledge is socially and historically constructed and reconstructed, and inevitably this knowledge can only ever be partial and forever in a state of flux. However, this does not mean that we can know nothing, indeed I would argue that knowing our uncertainty can free us from the constrictions and rigidity of previous ways of knowing. Richardson (1994: p. 517) argues:

> The core of postmodernism is the doubt that any method or theory, discourse or genre, tradition or novelty, has a universal and general claim as the 'right' or the privileged form of authoritative knowledge.

I make no claims for the knowledge generated from this research being either right or privileged. Further, I would not want to be seen as 'expert' on these women's lives. Rather this is simply one distinctive way of knowing, interpreting and (re)presenting the lives of the lesbian students involved in this research. Consequently, through employing a variety of conceptual tools we can centre lesbian lives and better critique the institution of compulsory heterosexuality.

In seeking to understand these students' lives in higher education it is important to locate them within a social and political context that largely

75

renders their presence both invisible and marginal. Section 28 of The Local Government Act of England and Wales (1988)[2] introduced by the last Conservative government to combat the twin threats of local government autonomy and homosexuality continues to be a powerful symbol of the prejudice of the last Parliament (and others) towards lesbian women and gay men. This repressive legislation carries powerful negative and stereotyped messages about homosexuality as a stigmatised and socially threatening identity. Section 28 thereby continues to legitimise and 'naturalize' hegemonic heterosexual discourses whilst at the same time defining, regulating, policing and enforcing sexual boundaries. Thus it is possible to be lesbian or gay only in specific places and spaces and further, clearly, only certain forms of behaviour are legally approved (see Bristow, 1989 and Clarke, 1998a).

Undoubtedly Section 28 has also had a marked effect on the teaching of lesbian and gay issues in schools and given the incidence of homophobic bullying in schools and the high rate of teenage suicide amongst lesbian and gay youth this is particularly concerning (see Douglas *et al.*, 1997). Moreover, the legislation has created a climate of fear amongst homosexual teachers (and students), the majority of whom are concerned for their continued (and future) employment should their sexual identity be revealed. Hence their perceived need to engage in heterosexual passing strategies and self-censorship in order to conceal their real lesbian and gay identities (see Clarke, 1997; Epstein, 1994).

It is pertinent to note that currently there is no specific legal protection for lesbian women and gay men who feel that they have been discriminated at work on the grounds of their sexual orientation. The Sex Discrimination Act is in the process of being amended and looks likely to include sexual orientation; further, European law about human rights is also under review. Nevertheless, "A review of homosexual teacher litigation in the USA since 1940, for example, portrays a judicial system unwilling to support the employment of gay and lesbian educators" (Harbeck, 1987, quoted in Woods, 1992: p. 91).

The locations of lesbian lives and the telling of life stories

This research draws on the life stories of nine white, able-bodied lesbian PE students. These life stories were gathered via interviews during the winter of 1994 which focused on segments of their lives and educative experiences. As such it follows that I accept Bertaux's (1981: p. 8) contention that the life story "need (not) cover the entire life-span and all its aspects.' In interpreting these life stories I draw like Plummer (1983) on other documents of life (for example personal correspondence) to gain a more complete picture of the complexities of lesbian lives. .

Life stories are more than just the telling of tales, they can as Beynon (1985: p. 165) argues "generate sensitizing concepts and contribute to conceptual frameworks and theory building". Accordingly we can learn (and theorise) about the self as well as the lives of those that we are researching. Life stories are therefore "important tools in research and in political change" (Plummer, 1983: p. 82). They are particularly valuable in that they are able to capture and uncover the contradictions and ambiguities, the complexities and tensions and the multilayers of lives that other methods may fail to reveal. Such detailed insights can provide us with a more encompassing view and in so doing it is possible to focus both on the specific as well as the general of lesbian lives.

Access to the students was difficult due to the prevailing climate of fear of exposure that surrounds lesbian (and gay) student teachers and forces many of them to remain an invisible and silent presence within higher education. Contact was initially made through a lesbian PE student teacher known to me, who contacted other lesbian student teachers at Acresdown University[3] to see if they were willing to talk to me in confidence about their lives. Contact was also made in this manner because such are the silences and the relative secrecy that it is not always possible to identify with any degree of certainty those women who are lesbian (see Squirrell, 1989). I contacted one of the participants (Dee) by telephone and she then arranged five other interviews for me. The students from Acresdown who were involved in the research were aged between 19 and 23 and came from a variety of working and middle class backgrounds. The length of time they had been at university varied, two were in their second year (Eddi and Fea) and four were in their fourth and final year of study (Adele, Berni, Christine and Dee). These six individual interviews all took place in the same student flat over a period of two days. All the participants selected a pseudonym, the only proviso being that they select any name with a specific letter so as to aid me with remembering the sequencing of the interviews. Hence at Acresdown the first interviewee's name began with an 'A', the second with a 'B' and so forth up to the letter 'F'. Glenwood Institute of Higher Education was the location for the next interview, this was with a fourth year student Gina who was aged 26. The final two interviews were conducted at Longmoor College of Higher Education, the first took place in a 'safe' house, as Helen who was 19 and in her second year of study, had not disclosed her sexual identity to all her flatmates. The last interview was conducted with Jay who was 22 and in her fourth year at Longmoor.

Prior to the interviews all the participants were sent a letter outlining the research process and the procedures to be adopted to protect their anonymity together with a copy of the interview schedule. For the purposes of this research the life story interviews focused on three main discussion areas, namely, lesbian identity, life in college, and teaching practice experiences including their relationships with pupils and teaching colleagues. Given that there was no comparable research on PE students to analyse, these topics arose from my reading of other researchers' work on lesbian teachers (see Griffin, 1991; Khayatt, 1992) together with my own experiences of teaching physical education for seven years in secondary schools in Southern England. However, the interview topics were discussed with a lesbian PE student teacher who made a small number of suggestions which resulted in minor changes to the phrasing of the questions.

Permission to tape record the interviews was sought and in all cases this was granted. The interviews lasted on average for 60 minutes. Following transcription the text was returned to the individual student for comment and alteration where appropriate. Additionally, the students were invited to make written comments about being involved in the research and/or about the actual process of the interview.

In seeking to make sense of the narratives it became apparent that there is "no binding theory of narrative, no standard set of procedures" (Rosenwald and Ochberg, 1993: p. 16). What I was looking for was a way to build theory from within rather than imposing from without, and in so doing I wanted an approach that would both respect and uncover the student's ways of knowing. Nevertheless, I recognise that interpretation is clearly affected and guided by the research goals which in this case were, to better understand the experiences of lesbian student teachers in higher education. Accordingly, I recognise the problematic and complex nature of interpretation and that it is "a political, contested and unstable process between the lives of the researchers and those of the researched" (Holland and Ramazanoglu, 1994: p. 127). Further, I accept that:

> there is no technique of analysis or methodological logic that can neutralize the social nature of interpretation. Feminist researchers can only try to explain the grounds on which selective interpretations have been made by making explicit the process of decision-making which produces the interpretation, and the logic of the method on which these decisions are based. (Holland and Ramazanoglu, 1994: p. 133)

My reading alerted me to new ways of looking at and interpreting the data. It also made me ask questions about my own life in schools. Therefore it is inevitable that the analysis/interpretation of these lesbian lives draws partly on my own experiences of teaching in secondary schools. Cotterill and Letherby (1993: p. 74) describe a similar approach to their research, they reveal how the lives of their research participants "are filtered through us and the filtered stories of our lives are present (whether we admit it or not) in our written accounts".

In order to find a framework that was flexible enough to respond to these concerns I employed a combination of hermeneutics and grounded theory. Erben (1996: p. 160) sees hermeneutics as:

> the theory or science of interpretation, and hermeneutical investi-
> gation is a method of analysis applicable to all forms of cultural life.
> For hermeneutical research, cultural life is regarded as a com-
> position of cultural texts. In the case of biography, a life or self is
> regarded as a text. The hermeneutical procedure is employed in
> biographical research to understand the narratives of lives.

The strength of hermeneutics lies in its appreciation of "both that which is interpreted and the interpreting self" (Erben, 1996: p. 172). Such a framework does not deny the presence and integral role of the researcher in the research process. Further, the emphasis is on arriving at what the events/experiences mean for the participants (see Glucksmann, 1994).

I was also attracted to the work of Glaser and Strauss (1967) on grounded theory and particularly their emphasis on "theory as process; that is theory as an ever-developing entity, not as a perfect product" (p. 32). Like others I do not view theory as something that is static, rather I see it as something that develops and is discovered both from within the research itself and also from without (see Scraton and Flintoff, 1992). I have tended to make use of grounded theory in a similar way to Faraday and Plummer (1979) insofar as I have combined it with analytic induction to build a comparative picture across the life stories I have obtained (see also Butt and Raymond, 1989; Plummer, 1983). Such an analytic process allows concepts to be derived from and grounded in the data generated (see Burgess, 1984, Robson, 1998). Accordingly I read the interview transcripts (and listened again to the tapes) many times in order to begin to make sense of them. In doing so the focus for analysis began to emerge and was sharpened, and in connection with this I found like Riessman (1993: p. 57) that "features of the discourse often 'jump out', stimulated by prior theoretical interests ...".

This revisiting coupled as I have indicated previously with my theoretical readings enabled me to rethink some of my concepts and ideas and to recognise like Plummer (1983: p. 133) that "Theorising comes in many forms ...". Thus for example I came to realise that issues of space were appropriate considerations in terms of understanding how certain locations impacted on the students and their need to conceal their lesbian identities in schools and the wider community. Additionally I made use of the discussion areas as focused on in the life story interviews.

For the purpose of this paper my attention is directed to the students' experiences of campus life and teaching practice.

Life on campus — safely out of the closet?

For many students campus life provides the opportunity for new freedoms away from the potential confines of the home. It is a safe location for some to discover and create (and for others the opportunity to confirm) their sexual identity as lesbian for the first time. For Fea, university was a saving grace since prior to commencing her studies she had resorted to drinking to escape, she commented:

> I felt really guilty about myself and I felt really bad that I shouldn't be like this, and ... it's wrong and so on. But as soon as I started to talk to people ... it is completely natural for me now, I see my girlfriends as anyone else will see their boyfriends.

It was at Acresdown for the first time that Fea truly accepted herself. She explained that:

> The main thing is how easy college has made it ... if I hadn't gone to college I think I might have cracked up by now ... It is like accepted at college ... it has really helped me, it is the best thing I have ever done, and I am really happy with myself now.

Further, she commented that in college she could "be really open about it" (her sexual identity) since all her friends knew and as she said they did not "have any hang-ups about it either". Christine revealed how she too was glad to have gone to Acresdown, for her it was the first time that she had (knowingly) met someone who was gay. She admitted that she was "really scared" and "wanted to run away because [I] ... didn't want to encounter anything new that put [me] ... in a position where [I] ... felt insecure. But as it was it didn't bother [me] ... at all." She said:

> It has [college] opened my eyes to an awful lot more things and I'm glad that I am away and [can] be more independent. I can get on with my life and sometimes I feel that I have a different life than maybe I do at home. I don't hide things, but I don't ... tell people some things that go on.

Such opportunities to confirm a lesbian identity are crucial if the hegemony of heterosexuality and the institution of compulsory heterosexuality is ultimately to be dismantled and so allow us all to create our own sexual landscapes.

Life on campus was in the main a comfortable place and space for these students to discover alternative ways of being themselves and where, as Fea pointed out "you don't have to put on any pretences any more." Jay saw Longmoor College as being a safe place to be, she believed that:

> ... in college it's a much ... close[r] environment and it's quite a sheltered environment ... and it means because there [are] quite a lot of you around it's almost like safety in numbers. People are a lot more open ... because you are not surrounded by parents and relatives and family, people can do basically what they want to do with only their peers around.

This 'safety in numbers' is also significant in that for many lesbians once they begin their teaching careers their concealment of their lesbian identity means that they remain isolated from other lesbian colleagues and as such they are denied the potential power and safety of a lesbian community and the sense of belonging that can be created through such membership (see Clarke, 1998a). Given too that these students recognise the need to conceal their lesbian identities when in school in order to successfully complete their teaching practice it becomes possible to understand why many are particularly anxious to take up employment close to where they have trained and where they know other lesbians. Thus, not only did college provide as Berni commented "a little sort of community", but it also meant that since there was a group of lesbians on one site that Dee did not "feel a bit freakish ... [as] there are a lot of people around." As she said "you know it is more acceptable and normal, than if you are one or two people in your year." Further, Berni commented:

> Everyone stays around here because it's just safe. There must be about two or three people that moved away and they've hated it ... [because] you've got to start all over again and it's not the same if you're straight ... you can just like 'oh I'll go out with you for a drink' ... [but] as well as building up your friendships enough to sort of come out to them ... you're constantly thinking do I trust them enough to tell them?

Another concern about returning 'home' was the perceived difficulty of fitting back into 'family life'. Christine commented:

> ... you can't do anything in our place, somebody always finds out
> about something, and it would get passed around ... and it is like
> too close for comfort in some ways for you to be who you are.

Whilst campus life, as we have seen, can open up new (sexual) freedoms it
can also bring increasing dangers, particularly insofar as these lesbian
students are now a visible presence on the largely heterosexual landscape,
hence they can more easily become potential targets for harassment and
abuse as is illustrated in the vignettes below. Further, given the contention
about their visible presence it would be a gross mistake to assume that all
campus life is safe. Thus, although it may appear from earlier comments
that the students were free to do what they wanted with whoever they
wished, the campus was also a hostile place to live and study in.

All nine of the students had at various times been subjected to verbal
abuse and harassment by their heterosexual peers[4]. Comments mostly
went unchallenged for fear of making the situation worse, although some of
the students at Acresdown stated that they would sit in the front row in
lectures in order to avoid comments being made at them and anyone
turning round and shouting 'lezzie' at them (Berni). For these students the
verbal abuse they were subjected to often took the form of homo/lesbo
phobic jokes as well as comments made about them as 'fucking queer'
individuals or as the 'lezzie group'. Adele for example described how the
'lads' would joke "how can you do without a man?" By and large it was felt
that the 'lads' were the main perpetrators of these insults and innuendo.
Berni stated that "the lads in our year can be a bit of a pain ...". Eddi also
felt that "mostly it is the lads that you get problems off"[5]. One of the
'problems' Eddi encountered was when one of the lads took her car keys.
This followed an incident in the college bar when, as she recalled one of the
lads said to:

> ...Ellie that plays hockey with us ... and [who] had been away for a
> weekend playing hockey ... "they are gay, you are, you must be
> because you hang around there".

Although Eddi had seen the lad take her keys she admitted that she "didn't
want to make a scene because [I] knew they knew about me and [I] just
wanted everything to keep quiet". Keeping quiet meant that she had to walk
home as she didn't have her car keys. She later got a call from the college
security guard to inform her that her car had been stolen by 'the lads' from
her year and been abandoned outside of Ellie's house. Eddi reasoned that
this incident was because she was lesbian and also that Ellie who was

heterosexual had "spent a lot of time with the hockey lot and not with him". Berni, in trying to explain why the lads behaved as they did, remarked:

> I think they feel really threatened by it and they can't come to terms with it ... and it's just like 'oh for god's sake we've been hearing this for four years can you not just give it a rest?' It gets really grating on your nerves.

Although as we have seen it was the lads who verbally abused these lesbian students, Christine pointed out that some of the 'girly girls' (i.e. those who were heterosexual), were on occasions rather 'bitchy' and likely to be abusive. Christine described how the "girly girls have always got boyfriends and their ... make up on". The issue at Acresdown was that these 'girly girls' were seen as the "worst ones for chatting" about the lesbians. At Longmoor it was the netball team that Helen felt caused "a lot of grief". Helen recalled how in a song that the netball club sang to the hockey club, "at the end they sing 'at least we shag the right sex'".

Like Stanley and Wise (1993: p. 88) I believe that:

> ... lesbians are oppressed because we are particularly threatening women — women who aren't dependent on men, and in this sense 'free women'. We feel that many men react to what they experience as threatening by 'sexualizing' it.

This 'sexualizing' was recounted in several of the interviews. The students felt that they were seen by their male peers as a real challenge to go out with as opposed to the lesser challenge of going out with a heterosexual student. Dee recalled how the lads had commented to one lesbian student that if she went out with them "it might do you good". Further, to this Fea outlined how she was approached by one of the lads who said "I can cure you ... come with me", she replied that she didn't want to be cured and told him to 'sod off'. She also described how "some lads in Berni's year ... were saying we'd like to go to bed with you, and we'll sort you out". Other students had had similar comments/suggestions made to them. Jay for example remembered how she had been sitting and chatting to one male student on a minibus when some of the lads passed and she:

> ... overheard one of them saying ... 'I don't know why you are bothering to talk to her you know she's not worth the fucking effort.'

For some of the students the situation got much worse when they were attacked on their way home from their last disco at college by a male student from the same college. Following the assault and trial the said male student was given a custodial sentence. One[6] of the students wrote to me about the incident reporting how:

> If this was ever to happen it probably happened at the best time. I was about to leave my cosy little nest and I hadn't realised how much college protected me. I had always argued that being honest and open about my sexuality was the correct thing to do but I realise now I had become too blinkered to what really happens. People can justify attacking others because they think [sic] you might be gay. At the moment I think I've taken a step back in my self because I always thought if people were educated about homo-sexuality and we were visible, in time they would not just get used to the idea but they'd actually accept it — it wouldn't be a question of hiding everything. However I can no longer believe that ...

These examples have but scraped the surface of the experiences of this group of lesbian students on campus and at this stage it is beyond the scope of this paper to explore them further. What is apparent is how homophobic and heterosexist discourses impact negatively upon their lives on campus. The following section examines their experiences whilst in secondary schools on teaching practice.

Life in schools and struggles for sexual identity

Teaching practice was both a time and location where different rules and expectations were encountered and where in some cases these 'codes' were in harsh contrast to the relatively protected environment of the college campus. Thus, these students had to learn how to negotiate a different terrain, be it in the staff room, gymnasium or in the wider school community. These adjustments were not without difficulty given that they were now moving to a more oppressive site compared to the previously comparatively liberatory campus site.

On teaching practice all the students to some extent built protective barriers around themselves in order to conceal their lesbian identity from both staff and pupils. Mechanisms for deceiving or diverting attention away from their personal lives were established so as not "to rock the boat in anyway" (Adele). These mechanisms included avoiding situations where they were likely to be asked personal questions (i.e. in the staffroom), and not mentioning the women they had been out with or the names of pubs/ clubs that they had visited which were known as being frequented by lesbian women. Helen for instance felt that:

> ... you can't say a thing and if they [teaching colleagues] ask you if
> you have been out last night, or where have you been, you have to
> lie about what pub you have been to or whatever.

Such actions were not too dissimilar to those engaged in by lesbian PE
teachers (see Clarke, 1996 and Squires and Sparkes, 1996).

Self censorship and denial were seen as necessary for survival. The
contrast between life in college and school is marked, Dee commented
about her life in college:

> ... here you don't have to bother about what you say or how you act
> really. There are obvious limits, but you don't have to be worried
> about being seen with somebody all the time. It is much easier, I
> think it is TP [teaching practice] that hammers it into you. When
> you are out in schools you think this is what it is going to be like ...
> it is quite scary.

Despite the fact that they were not necessarily in school for long periods of
time in which to build up relationships with staff and perhaps therefore less
likely to enter into prolonged conversations about home life, they all were
nevertheless concerned about being questioned about their life outside of
the school environment. The fear of the revelation of their lesbian identity
and the impact that this might have on their future job prospects/career
was constantly at the back of their minds as they strove to get everything
up to scratch (i.e. lesson plans, evaluations, units of work and teaching
practice files) in order to pass their teaching practice. Such pressures and
experiences provided a stark contrast to the relative openness with which
they could lead their lives within the campus environment.

Compulsory heterosexuality remains the order of the day in the
schooling world and these lesbian PE student teachers were 'forced' to
comply in order not to disturb the status quo and thereby bring unwelcome
attention to their carefully concealed sexual identity. Christine, for
instance, when going for a meal with the PE department at the end of her
school practice described how she was asked by the female head of
department if she was going to bring somebody to 'the do'. When she replied
that she wasn't, the teacher said to her "haven't you got a boyfriend then?".
Christine admitted that she hadn't and was then told by this same teacher
"well don't bring a woman". Christine described how she replied:

> I am not going to bring a woman and she said 'well I am just telling
> you don't.' ... A week later she said 'bring yourself a man'. She had
> a hang up about me bringing a woman.

In order to both protect and conceal their lesbian identities the students also felt obliged to listen to homophobic comments and slurs made by other teachers. Dee admitted that she found it hard to laugh at jokes made about homosexuals. If an acceptable and socially sanctioned (heterosexual) identity is to be constructed and maintained the students believed that the temptation to challenge had to be resisted so as to reduce the risk of possible exposure. Berni remembered how she had been in a school when they were appointing a 'new' Head of Department and the male teacher commented "well they want a woman ... that means they'll either be a blond bimbo or a lesbian hockey player". Christine recalled an incident in her school when a comment was made about her college teaching practice supervisor "oh we know her, she's gay". Christine explained how:

> ... they make a big deal [of it] saying 'oh the poof is coming today' and you laugh and joke with people don't you and you don't say that you can't say that about somebody, ... sometimes it is easier ... just to let them say what they want because you don't want to upset them ... I tend to let people continue because it is more hassle than it's worth.

Acceptance of these remarks becomes a way of surviving and negotiating the hostile school terrain.

Changing rooms — another site of struggle

Given that the body is dominant in PE there was much fear amongst the students over supervising pupils showering and changing. The very physicality of the subject clearly poses an additional threat to the revelation of their lesbian identity and leaves them wary as to how they are likely to be perceived by others (teachers and pupils alike). The gendered bodily culture of physical education creates a unique context for the denial and camouflage of a lesbian identity that might not be experienced by students (and teachers) within other subject disciplines. Berni explained that she:

> ... hate(d) supervising the kids going in the showers. I mean it's just really stupid but you just feel really awkward about it and they're like going 'oh you're looking at me Miss' and stuff like that and you just find yourself being just doubly sort of not looking.

This concern was also shared by Christine who remarked:

I had no desire for any of the kids, nothing like that but if people knew you were gay, you know watching young girls in the showers you could cause yourself so much hassle ... you have got a lost cause if people know that you are gay, you are as good as guilty before you've done anything ... I thought if people knew they would be saying 'don't let her in those shower rooms'.

These concerns were also paramount in the minds of lesbian PE teachers (see Clarke, 1996; Squires and Sparkes, 1996) and meant that for them, too, the daily routine of supervising pupils in changing rooms becomes a situation to be safely negotiated.

Several of the students remembered how during their schooldays they used to call their PE teachers 'lezzie' or 'lez' or 'lesbian'. Similar labelling was also often overheard when they were in schools. Dee described the reaction of a teacher at the school she was on teaching practice at as follows:

This teacher went absolutely off her head, and I was thinking what's your problem? Kids are always going to find something to say about you, whether it is true, you are a PE teacher and you should expect it. They always say it, whether you have been married for 25 years or got 10 children ... PE is always linked to it ... I couldn't understand why this teacher was so horrified, it seemed to me that this is the worst thing that anybody had said about her.

These vignettes illustrate a number of key issues, firstly how lesbian PE students may come to internalise negative stereotypes about themselves based on their sexual identity, as well as accepting the inevitability of these being levelled at them. Secondly, it demonstrates how PE students/ teachers are 'fair' game for targeting by pupils; and, thirdly, it illustrates how the word lezzie was a powerful weapon to be used against female teachers/students regardless of their sexual identity. This depressing picture is not uncommon within the conservative world of PE and sport. Traditionally the world of sport has been viewed as a male domain that women enter at their peril and by doing so they run the risk of being tagged with the pejorative label 'lesbian'. As Woods (1992: p. 91) argues, "to be athletic is equated with masculinity and masculine women are labelled as lesbian. Therefore, athletic women are stereotyped as lesbian". Physical education students (and teachers) are especially vulnerable to such myths and stereotypes (see Clarke, 1996; Woods and Harbeck, 1992). Further, students are particularly vulnerable given that if they do not pass teaching practice they will fail to get a teaching post and additionally a poor report would adversely affect their job prospects.

Concluding remarks

This research has revealed a partial picture of the experiences of these lesbian PE student teachers and in so doing it has illustrated that whilst some terrains enable the establishment of relatively safe havens where a lesbian identity can be publicly displayed, others are dangerous places for the open display of a lesbian identity. Accordingly, it is no wonder that these students employ various strategies in school to pass as heterosexual. Nevertheless, it should be recognised that these students were not always passive and subjugated persons, they did challenge and resist in a number of significant ways. Indeed, it can be contended that just being lesbian, publicly or privately, can be deemed as an act of resistance in a heterosexist and homophobic world. In connection with this Cheryl Clarke (1983: p. 128) makes the case that "No matter how a woman lives out her lesbianism — in the closet, in the state legislature, in the bedroom — she has rebelled ...". Further, I am in agreement with Bok (1986: p. 19) that "To be able to hold some information about oneself or to channel it and thus influence how one is seen by others gives power ...". Thus, to pass as heterosexual is, as Dhairyam (1994: p. 43) indicates "to enjoy a purchase in power". Hence passing may provide access (and infiltration) to certain heterosexual privileges and provide a degree of security and freedom in certain locations and situations and moreover it may mean that a lesbian existence actually survives and continues.

For some of the lesbian students their silences (and non-challenging of homophobic remarks) were a way of fighting back. As Jay claimed, "If you ignore it then they never actually know ... I've just sort of said 'sod you, you don't deserve to know'". Such actions may be interpreted as another powerful form of resistance and defence. Bensimon (1992) asserts that silence may be the only form of resistance that is open to some lesbian women in the educational system. By remaining silent Bensimon (1992: p. 109) argues that heterosexuals are deprived of:

> ... the satisfaction that derives from showing understanding and tolerance of the 'negative other' without conceding how their own heterosexual privilege contributes to the structures that make lesbian existence oppressive.

The issue of silence is complex, as are other forms of resistance, all seem to have the capacity for contradiction and contestation. As we have seen resistance is not easy. To be openly lesbian (or gay) on campus remains a struggle against heterosexual normativity. Accordingly, we need to be wary of prematurely celebrating such acts, since resistance does not necessarily lead to transformation of the social, sexual and spatial landscape.

Notes

1   This is not to deny that there are many forms of feminist scholarship, but here I make specific use of Jeffreys' (1990; 1994) conceptions of lesbian feminism. Such a conception centres lesbian experiences and begins from their lives by calling the 'naturalness' of heterosexuality into doubt. From this perspective heterosexuality is viewed as a political institution which needs to be brought to an end in the interests of all women's freedom and sexual self determination (Jeffreys, 1994).

2   Section 28 of the Local Government Act (1988) of England and Wales stated:

(1) A local authority shall not —
(a) intentionally promote homosexuality or publish material with the intention of promoting homosexuality;
(b) promote the teaching in any maintained school of the acceptability of homosexuality as a pretended family relationship.
Nothing in subsection (1) above shall be taken to prohibit the doing of anything for the purpose of treating or preventing the spread of disease.

The passing of Section 28 can be seen as an attempt to restore the family to its 'rightful' place at the heart of British life, to protect it from attack by lesbians and gay men and to reassert the 'moral' high ground in schools. Although Section 28 has been summarily dismissed as ambiguously worded it remains as Colvin and Hawksley (1989: Back cover) claim "dangerously open to misinterpretation, its implications are potentially far-reaching". For further discussion of the impact of Section 28 see Clarke, 1996.

3   All HEI names are pseudonyms. The Universities/Higher Education Institutes (HEIs) that the students attended were located in a city or large town.

4   The evidence of the alarming incidence of campus discrimination, harassment and hate crimes against lesbian and gay students has been well documented by D'Augelli (1989a) and Herek (1989) in the United States and by Trenchard and Warren (1987) and Fahey (1993) in England.

5   D'Augelli (1989b) and Clift (1989) also found in their research that male
    students had more negative and less tolerant attitudes towards lesbians
    and gay students than their female counterparts.

6   I have intentionally omitted any name here in order to further protect
    the identity of the student as her parents were unaware that this assault
    had occurred.

References

D'Augelli, A.R. (1989a) 'Lesbians' and gay men's experiences of discrimination
    and harassment in a university community', *American Journal of
    Community Psychology*, 17, 3: pp. 317–321.

———— (1989b) 'Homophobia in a university community: views of prospective
    research assistants', *Journal of College Student Development*, No. 30
    (November): pp. 546–552.

Bensimon, E. (1992) 'Lesbian existence and the challenge to normative
    constructions of the academy', *Journal of Education*, Vol. 174, No. 3: pp.
    98–113.

Bertaux, D. (ed) (1981) *Biography and society: The life history approach in the
    social sciences*. London, Sage.

Beynon, J. (1985) 'Institutional change and career histories in a compre-
    hensive school', in S. J. Ball and I. F. Goodson (eds) *Teachers' lives and
    careers*. Lewes: The Falmer Press.

Bok, S. (1986) *Secrets: On the ethics of concealment and revelation*. Oxford:
    Oxford University Press.

Bristow, J. (1989) 'Being gay: politics, identity, pleasure', *New Formations*, No.
    9: pp. 61–68.

Burgess, R.G. (1984) *In the field: an introduction to field research*. London:
    Allen and Unwin.

Butt, R.L. and Raymond, D. (1989) 'Studying the nature and development of
    teachers' knowledge using collaborative autobiography', *International
    Journal of Educational Research*, Vol. 13, No. 4: pp. 403–419.

Clarke, C. (1983) 'Lesbianism: an act of resistance', in C. Moraga and G.
    Anzaldua (eds) *This bridge called my back: Writings by radical women of
    color*. New York: Kitchen Table, Women of Color Press.

Clarke, G. (1995) 'Outlaws in sport and education? Exploring the sporting and
    education experiences of lesbian physical education teachers', in
    L. Lawrence, E. Murdoch and S. Parker (eds) *Professional and Develop-
    ment Issues in Leisure, Sport and Education* (LSA Publication No. 56).
    Eastbourne, Leisure Studies Association, pp. 45–58.

—— (1996) 'Conforming and contesting with (a) difference: how lesbian students and teachers manage their identities', *International Studies in Sociology of Education*, 6, 2: pp. 191–209.

—— (1997) 'Playing a part: the lives of lesbian physical education teachers', in G. Clarke and B. Humberstone (eds) *Researching women and sport*. London: Macmillan.

—— (1998a) 'Working out: Lesbian teachers and the politics of (dis)location', *Journal of Lesbian Studies*, 2, 4: pp. 85–99.

—— (1998b) Voices from the margins: lesbian teachers in physical education, Unpublished PhD thesis, Leeds Metropolitan University.

Clift, S. M. (1989) 'Lesbian and gay issues in education: a study of the attitudes of first year students in a college of higher education', *British Educational Research Journal*, 14, 1: pp. 31–50.

Colvin, M. with Hawksley, J. (1989) *Section 28: a practical guide to the law and its implications*. London: National Council for Civil Liberties.

Cotterill, P. and Letherby, G. (1993) 'Weaving stories: personal auto/biographies in feminist research', *Sociology*, 27, 1: pp. 67–79.

Dhairyam, S. (1994) 'Racing the lesbian, dodging white critics' in L. Doan (ed) *The lesbian postmodern*. New York, Columbia University Press.

Douglas, N., Warwick, I., Kemp, S. and Whitty, G. (1997) *Playing it safe: responses of secondary school teachers to lesbian, gay and bisexual pupils, bullying, HIV and AIDS education and Section 28*. Health and Education Research Unit, University of London, Institute of Education.

Epstein, D. (ed) (1994) *Challenging lesbian and gay inequalities in education*. Buckingham: Open University Press.

Erben, M. (1996) 'The purposes and processes of biographical method', in D. Scott and R. Usher (eds) *Understanding educational research*. London: Routledge.

Erben, M. (ed) (1998) *Biography and education: An edited Collection*. London: Falmer Press.

Fahey, W. S. (1993) Lesbian and gay men's experiences of peer discrimination and harassment in higher education. Unpublished paper.

Faraday, A. and Plummer, K. (1979) 'Doing life histories', *Sociological Review*, Vol. 27, No. 4: pp. 773–798.

Glaser, B.G. and Strauss, A.L. (1967) *The discovery of grounded theory: Strategies for qualitative research*. New York: Aldine Publishing Company.

Glucksmann, M. (1994) 'The work of knowledge and the knowledge of women's work', in M. Maynard and J. Purvis (eds) *Researching women's lives from a feminist perspective*. London: Taylor and Francis.

Griffin, P. (1991) 'Identity management strategies among lesbian and gay educators', *Qualitative Studies in Education*, Vol. 4, No. 3: pp. 189–202.

Herek, G.M. (1989) 'Hate crimes against lesbian and gay men. Issues for research and policy', *American Psychologist*, Vol. 44, No. 6: pp. 948–955.

Holland, J. and Ramazanoglu, C. (1994) 'Coming to conclusions: power and interpretation in the researching young women's sexuality', in M. Maynard and J. Purvis (eds) *Researching women's lives from a feminist perspective*. London: Taylor and Francis.

Jeffreys, S. (1990) *Anticlimax: a feminist perspective on the sexual revolution*. London: The Women's Press.

———— (1994) *The lesbian heresy: A feminist perspective on the lesbian sexual revolution*. London: The Women's Press.

Khayatt, D. (1992) *Lesbian teachers: An invisible presence*. Albany, State University of New York Press.

Mac an Ghail, M. (1991) 'Schooling, sexuality and male power; towards an emancipatory curriculum', *Gender and Education*, Vol. 3, 3: 291–309.

Plummer, K. (1983) *Documents of life. An introduction to the problems and literature of a humanistic method*. London: Unwin Hyman.

———— (1989) 'Lesbian and gay youth in England', *Journal of Homosexuality*, Vol. 17, No. 3–4: pp. 195–223.

Richardson, L. (1994) 'Writing: A method of inquiry', in N. K. Denzin and Y. S. Lincoln (eds) *Handbook of qualitative research*. London: Sage.

Riessman, C.K. (1993) *Narrative analysis*. London: Sage.

Robson, C. (1998) *Real world research: A resource for social scientists and practitioner-researchers*. Oxford: Blackwell.

Rosenwald, G. C. and Ochberg, R. L. (1992) 'Introduction: life stories, cultural politics, and self-understanding', in G. C. Rosenwald and R. L. Ochberg (eds) *Storied lives: The cultural politics of self-understanding*. New Haven and London: Yale University Press.

Scraton, S. and Flintoff, A. (1992) 'Feminist research and physical education', in A. C. Sparkes (ed) *Research in physical education and sport; exploring alternative visions*. London: Falmer Press.

Shilling, C. (1991) 'Social space, gender inequalities and educational differentiation', *British Journal of Sociology of Education*, Vol. 12, No. 1: pp. 23–44.

Squires, S.L. and Sparkes, A. C. (1996) 'Circles of silence: sexual identity in physical education and sport', *Sport, Education and Society*, Vol. 1, No. 1: pp. 77–101.

Squirrell, G. (1989) 'Teachers and issues of sexual orientation', *Gender and Education*, Vol. 1, No. 1: pp. 17–34.

Stanley, L. and Wise, S. (1993) *Breaking out again: Feminist ontology and epistemology*. London: Routledge.

Trenchard, L. and Warren, H. (1987) 'Talking about school: the experiences of young lesbians and gay men', in G. Weiner and M. Arnot (eds) *Gender under scrutiny: new inquiries in education*. London: Unwin Hyman.

Woods, S. (1992) 'Describing the experiences of lesbian physical educators: a phenomenological study', in A.C. Sparkes (ed) *Research in physical education and sport: Exploring alternative visions*. London: The Falmer Press.

Woods, S. and Harbeck, K. (1992) 'Living in two worlds: the identity management strategies used by lesbian and gay educators', in K. Harbeck (ed) *Coming out of the classroom closet: Gay and lesbian students, teachers and curricula*. New York: Harrington Park Press.

Football in the UK:
Women, Tomboys, Butches and Lesbians

Jayne Caudwell

Centre for Leisure and Sport Research,
Leeds Metropolitan University (UK)

Introduction

This paper explores gender as it relates to women who play football in the UK. The discussion will draw on relevant gender theory as it has appeared within sport sociology, feminist political thought, and cultural studies. In particular, it will offer an analysis of the figure of 'the butch' and tomboyism. In short, the paper considers sport and female masculinity. It is my intention to challenge the notion that masculinity in girls and women is abhorrent and pathological.

Reference to 'tomboy' and 'butch' have appeared regularly in both the qualitative and quantitative research material of my current research. The qualitative research material represents 437 completed postal question-naires. 870 questionnaires were sent out to all clubs registered in 9 of the 10 regional leagues (England and Wales only) and the British University Student's Association (BUSA); the sample was not random but geographically selected. The questionnaire data documents the socio-demographic details of women playing in England and Wales during the season 1997/8. Some of the findings from the quantitative research will be used here to support the qualitative research material. The qualitative research represents 14 semi structured, in depth interviews with women who were playing football at the time of interview (seasons 1997/8 and 1998/9). The topic guide for the interviews has two distinct sections. The first section considers football generally and the second section focuses specifically on players' understanding of sexuality and the relationships between football and sexuality.

Femininity and masculinity

It has been argued that the sociology of sport and physical activity, as it has developed over the last 30 years, reflects an analytical and theoretical shift from the sociology of men's sport to a focus on gender (Hall, 1990; Whitson, 1990). Initially this focus on gender was understood to represent women, femininity and sport. In other words a feminist analysis of the position of women within sport's gendered relations. However, more recently this focus on gender and gender relations has incorporated an analysis of men and masculinity (for example see Anderson, 1999; Baker and Boyd, 1997; Messner and Sabo, 1990; Spracklen, 1995; Whannel, 1998; Wheaton, 1998). To date, commentators have considered femininity and masculinity independently, co dependently, and almost exclusively as components of gender relations. It is worth noting here that within such analyses the body has remained an important anchor and site for discussion. Increasingly, the nuances contained within the 'categories' femininity and masculinity are being intentionally documented. By introducing gender as multiple, writers are beginning to question the paucity of the existing gender classification. This is particularly evident within the writing on masculinities (Boyd, 1997; Whannel, 1998; Wheaton, 1998). However, there is limited in-depth analysis which explores gender transitivity, which is according to Eve Sedgwick (1990) "the feminized man or virilized woman" (p. 42). There is literature which attempts to dispel "the myth of masculinisation of the female athlete" (Fasting and Scraton, 1997), however there is no existing literature within sport sociology which offers a detailed analysis of and/or unpacks gender variance. In comparison such work exists within cultural studies and continues apace. For example, Judith Halberstam (1998) offers one of the few accounts which fully explores female masculinity. Halberstam argues that her book is a serious and committed attempt "to make masculinity safe for women and girls" (p. 268). By "safe", Halberstam means functional and "acceptable". The relevance of her work to this paper is the contribution it makes to a discussion on: the embodiment of gender; the butch; and the tomboy.

Especially within sport, and also within active leisure, the feminine and masculine have been theorised from a position which privileges notions of embodiment and corporeality.

> It may be suggested that masculinizing and feminizing practices associated with the body are at the heart of the social construction of masculinity and femininity and that this is precisely why sport matters in the total structure of gender relations. (Whitson, 1990: p. 23/24)

The impact of physical activity on the 'outer' body can be very visible: firm, lean, taut, muscular bodies. The exercising body functions within a particular economic environment and in 'Western' society the commodification of both, sport and active leisure and the body, is more than apparent. Flintoff, Scraton and Bramham (1995) claim "the media and cultural industries sustain icons of the powerful body for each gender: the masculine muscular body and the feminine toned body" (p. 93). In fact, the notion of a 'feminine toned body' arguably collapses the feminine/masculine distinction, as women with muscle challenge the "tenuous equation established between masculinity, muscularity, and men" (Holmlund, 1997: p. 154). Jennifer Hargreaves (1997) cites Susan Bordo's (1990) contention that "in recent years the athletic and muscular image of femininity, although quite solid and bulky looking, has become highly desirable" (p. 40). Leena St Martin and Nicola Gavey (1996) also refer to Susan Bordo's (1993) acclaim that "a slim body is no longer sufficient, the normative feminine ideal must be muscularly developed as well" (p. 46). These shifting constructs of embodied femininity and masculinity impact on gender relations and define our understanding of what it means to be a woman or a man.

(Not) To look like a woman

Traditionally sport and active leisure have tended to reify and naturalise the conventional gender 'categories' of femininity and masculinity; this has been particularly so within the physical education system (Scraton, 1987, 1992; Parker, 1996). Research has focused on how femininity and masculinity have been constructed and hyperbolised within sport and active leisure culture and ideology (Whitson, 1990; Bryson, 1987) and how gender is regulated to the extent that femininity and masculinity are codified and inexorable. This is made evident by Susan Birrell and Cheryl Cole (1994) in their study which explores "the implications of the entrance of Renee Richards, a constructed-female transsexual, into the women's professional tennis circuit" (p. 1). Birrell and Cole argue that "sport functions as a major site for the naturalization of sex and gender differences" (p. 18). They show how transsexualism disturbs the neat, 'logical' and 'naturalised' notions surrounding sex, gender, identity and the body. They argue that the treatment of Renee Richards not only reveals the social construction of gender, "but the social construction of the sex-gender connection" (p. 18). They show how sport ideology produces a narrative which gives meaning to gender and notions of 'naturalised' sex. However, their analysis stops at a critique of sex differences and the sex-gender connection, it is apparent that they do not engage with the idea that 'men's' sport and 'women's' sport, as based on obvious sex differences, are the product of gendered presumption and not the base. In other words, there is no analysis of how 'men's' sport and 'women's' sport are constructed and/or produced.

To return to the idea of 'not to look like a woman', more recently research has focused on women's expanding involvement in sport and active leisure previously defined as male and therefore masculine. Women's participation in football, rugby, boxing and the like, impacts on 'naturalised' femininity and masculinity. The shift towards these sports by women affects the currency of the conventional gender distinction traditional to sport and active leisure. For instance, despite the trend towards female muscularity, women's involvement in 'traditional' male sports continues to challenge the gender logic underpinning sport's culture. Specific analysis which addresses this point is most evident within the literature on women bodybuilders.

Feminists (Holmlund, 1997; Kuhn, 1995; St Martin and Gavey, 1996), sociologists (Aoki, 1996) and those writing from within sport studies (Hall, 1996; Pugh, 1995), have made efforts to theorise women bodybuilders. The relevance here of such work is the unavoidable focus on embodied notions of gender and ideas surrounding the abject body qua femininity/masculinity. These themes are significant more generally when considering women's active involvement in activities and sports deemed male and masculine, and thus inappropriate for women to take part in. This ideology of inappropriateness is based on naturalised and obdurate notions of the feminine and masculine.

> The question of 'female muscle' however may only be 'in' in the 'right' aesthetic context and on the 'right' body. This has proven to be a crucial point in the possible acceptance of women in non-traditional sports. (Pugh, 1995: p. 80)

Women's active involvement in activities such as football, rugby and boxing follow in the wake of the feminist critique of the powerful gender relations evident within sport and leisure. Sport and leisure feminists have clearly challenged gendered notions as they relate to women's freedom and constraint. However, there has been limited feminist scrutiny of new concepts of femininity; femininity as plural; or disavowed femininity/masculinity, apart from the existing work on women bodybuilders. The work on women bodybuilders is interesting in the sense that it can not help but focus on the feminine and masculine. Specific questions that are raised by women choosing to build an overtly muscular body include: are women "rejecting femininity in favour of masculinity?" (Pugh, 1995: p. 80); does the body become "so extremely muscular that it can only be seen as 'masculine'" (Kuhn, 1995: p. 67), that is she looks like a 'man' (Aoki, 1996).

Similarly, issues surrounding endangered femininity are apparent within boxing. Through her analysis, Halberstam (1998) shows how female masculinity in boxers is abhorred and stigmatised to such an extent that women who participate "attempt to turn the gaze away from their potential masculinity" (p. 270). Jennifer Hargreaves (1997) also provides an analysis of boxing as a site where women feel obliged to assert their femininity. She cites Deirdre Gogarty: "I used to hang a punch bag in the cupboard and bang away at it when no-one was around (...) because I was afraid people would think I was weird and unfeminine" (p. 45). It is worth noting here that a depletion in femininity, that is to 'look like a man', does not always rely on muscularity, women who play sports such as football and rugby embody masculinity in less overt ways compared to body builders and boxers. However, in all cases the corporeal masculinisation of women incites notions of women's exercising bodies as abject bodies. Interestingly but not surprisingly given the focus of her work, Halberstam (1998) reads this relationship between the body and gender in reverse; "female-bodied people, must be forced into these abject genders" (p. 273).

Sport and active leisure clearly have an overwhelming regulatory influence on femininity and masculinity and gendered body motif. Femininity and masculinity are constructed in relation to sex, and sport and active leisure codify both sex and gender. Relevant to this analysis, Judith Butler (1993: p. xi) asks an important question and one which I will engage with during the discussion on tomboyism and the 'category' butch.

> Given this understanding of construction as constitutive constraint, is it still possible to raise the critical question of how such constraints not only produce the domain of intelligible bodies, but produce as well a domain of unthinkable, abject, unliveable bodies?

Gender and sexuality

Here I will show how gender and sexuality have been conflated to support a pathological theory of gender dysphoria, and how this collapsing of gender and sexuality has been read as a sign of aberrant sexuality. In particular, how female masculinity has been "annexed indisputably to lesbianism" (Halberstam, 1998: p. 54).

The late 1800s have been a period marked as the birth of "homosexuality as we know it today" (Foucault, cited in Sedgwick, 1990: p. 44). From the late nineteenth century and early twentieth century 'homosexuality' was defined and coded by a predominantly male language, theory and tradition. Sexologists such as Hirschfield, Krafft-Ebing, Ellis and later Freud used gender cues to assess and describe sexual identity. The 'medical experts' developed a medical discourse which squashed multiple expressions of gender variance and sexual variance into a narrow range of categories (Halberstam, 1998). Foucault (1980) argues that such an approach transformed sexual acts, "through complex discursive practices into stable notions of identity" (quoted in Halberstam, 1998, p. 75). In this way, sexology established a medical model of homosexuality based on gender role and object choice. Within the model, Eve Sedgwick's (1990) notion of a virile women is collapsed into the image of the 'mannish' lesbian; mannishness in women became inextricably linked to lesbianism. Esther Newton (1991) believes this conflation of gender role, gender identity and sexual orientation reflected a reluctance, by sexologists, to acknowledge active lust in women. Not only lesbians but also heterosexual women, who adopted a "language of lust" (Newton, 1991: p. 285), were viewed as deviant. Since active sexual desire was considered 'masculine' then, lesbians actively involved in sexual relationships with other women were not only seen as deviant, but also 'inverted'. Nineteenth century discourse on sexuality constructed the profound link between masculinity and the sexual, this meant the female invert "could not be classified as an asexual, 'normal' woman" (Gibson, 1997: p. 122), hence the lesbian became marked as 'pseudo-man'.

Physicians, such as Krafft-Ebing and Ellis, frequently and persistently listed evidence of masculinity in habits, abilities and features as relevant 'facts' indicating inversion in women. Ellis refers to well developed muscles, and Krafft-Ebing cites childhood enjoyment of masculine pastimes as signs of inversion (Gibson, 1997). Both 'characteristics' can be shown to have a direct relationship with participation in physical activity. More specifically, Krafft-Ebing offers a means to identify what he refers to as Uranism (a term devised by Ulrichs):

> Uranism may nearly always be suspected in females wearing their hair short, or who dress in the fashion of men, or pursue the sports and pastimes of their male acquaintances. (quoted in Munt, 1998: p. 62)

Similarly, Ellis's work characterises lesbians as having a "dislike and sometimes incapacity for needlework and other domestic occupations, while there is often some capacity for athletics" (quoted in Miller, 1995: p. 19). This notion of the 'authentic' lesbian as active and therefore masculine, was highly influential at the time and continued to be significant during the early twentieth century. For instance, in Radclyffe Hall's books *Miss Ogilvy Finds Herself* (1926) and *The Well of Loneliness* (1927), the characters — Miss Ogilvy and Stephen, "both occupy themselves with weight lifting and sports in their childhood" (Halberstam, 1998, p. 84). In particular, Stephen's inversion was portrayed most clearly when the character was taking part in sports such as horse riding and fencing. The depiction of Miss Ogilvy and Stephen as sportswomen functions as confirmation of their inversion.

Clearly lesbian sexuality has been constructed in a way which priorises the masculine over the feminine. According to Emma Healey (1996):

> There is no easy moment in history when an 'invert' became a 'butch', but it is the linking of the butch both to manliness and manly behaviour and to the medicalised and pathologised invert, that makes the butch such a contentious figure in our lesbian history. (p. 24)

Traditionally the 'butch' is vilified, maligned and condemned, and within feminist politics especially this figure has caused endless dispute. The intersection of butch/femme culture and feminism during the 1960s has been documented in a variety of ways (for example, see Feinberg, 1993; Nestle, 1989; and Roof, 1998). Leslie Feinberg's novel *Stone Butch Blues* powerfully articulates a social history of working class lesbian culture in America immediately prior to, and during the emergence of the Women's Liberation Movement. The account shows how the butch lesbian, irrespective of her politics, was alienated by an emerging feminist movement which linked masculinity to oppression and domination. By weaving together two periods of time, pre and post Stonewall (Stonewall represents the gay and lesbian 'fight backs' during the 1969 police raids on bars in Greenwich Village, New York), Feinberg illustrates how butches, regardless of the emerging human rights campaigns and shifts toward equal rights, continued to receive the most severe instances of discrimination and abuse.

Constructing gender

Feminist politics which have relied on, and continue to rely on, the alignment of sex and gender have not embraced the notion of female masculinity. The formulation of the sex/gender distinction during early 'second wave' feminist politics focused on gender as a construct. A critical theory of gender developed alongside and within theories of patriarchy. In short, the feminist analysis of the sex/gender distinction exposes the arrangement by which the sexed body, that is biological sex, receives a gender inscription. Here, sex is theorised as within the biological realm and gender as the effect of culture, thus the two are distinct. The cultural and social construction of gender marks women as feminine and men as masculine. Within patriarchal theory it is men, but more specifically traits of masculinity, which are central to the debate on women's oppression. Hence masculinity is positioned as an anathema. Clearly from this feminist position the adoption of a masculine style by women is problematic. For instance, some lesbian feminists (radical and revolutionary) have strongly rejected the idea of a gendered identity for lesbians. This adversity is argued as the political refusal to imitate, 'copy' hetero patriarchy. And so, the butch/femme lesbian culture most evident in the 50s, 60s and early 70s, with its gendered behaviours and identifications, is viewed by traditional lesbian feminists as "regressive and anti-political" (Roof, 1998). The butch identity is seen as a "manifestation of male sexual power" (Healey, 1996: p. 34), while the femme identity is written off as wholly duped and culturally constrained.

More recently, and in conjunction with the emerging Queer movement, there appears to be a contemporary celebration of the butch image within aspects of lesbian culture, lesbian politics and feminist politics. The ongoing debate within lesbian politics on the sexualised/desexualised nature of lesbian sexuality has generated a more detailed analysis of butch/femme lesbian culture and 'lesbian gender' (see work by Sally Munt, 1998a). Feminists and lesbians who have challenged the linear relationship between sex, gender, and desire, have offered accounts which argue for further detachment of sex and gender, and a rethinking of the ownership of desire. It is the sex/gender debates which are of particular relevance to the reading of the figure of the butch in this paper, in particular a post structuralist perspective.

Judith Butler's (1990 and 1993) analysis of the sex/gender distinction offers a radical rethinking of both sex and gender. She considers gender as socially and culturally constructed, however she challenges the anchoring of gender on the sexed body and questions the privileged positioning of the heterosexual matrix within which gender and the sexed body function. According to Butler (1990) sex and gender do not have to be viewed as mutually dependent. In fact it is the ideological construction of gender on the sexed body which gains intelligibility;

> The presumption of a binary gender system implicitly retains the belief in a mimetic relation of gender to sex whereby gender mirrors sex or is otherwise restricted by it. (p. 6)

Butler suggests that it is within a regime of heterosexuality that the gender dualism has real currency; as such, gender becomes obdurate and the product of a "hetero reality" (Whelehan, 1995: p. 206). Butler suggests that this 'naturalising' of gender is achieved through heterosexual hegemony. She argues that gender is fictitious, but becomes set by a series of imitations. According to Butler both femininity and masculinity are copies of copies, however the configurations of the feminine and masculine are legitimated and validated as authentic through a power field she identifies as the heterosexual matrix.

Butler's questioning of the proposal that gender signifies sex and her claim that sex is in fact also constructed through this signification, challenges structuralist feminist grand narrative. Her post structuralist reading of both sex and gender de-stabilise the assumption that women experience oppression and domination exclusively as a result of men and masculinity. As other feminists have illustrated women experience oppression and domination in many different ways, for example bell hooks (1990) shows how race intersects with gender.

Butler's reading of gender, positions masculinity and femininity as social constructs which can be deconstructed and reconstructed. This type of analysis offers a poststructuralist account of subjectivity and makes links with a Foucauldian interpretation of power. That is, that individuals as agents do not suffer oppression under an all prevailing structure of domination but experience their subjectivity within a charged 'power field'. The circulatory and discursive nature of this 'power field' gives rise to dominant forms of oppression i.e.. sexism, racism and heterosexism, these are historically and culturally specific. So, for example the denigrating and oppressive treatment of the butch, by sexologists and some strands of early second wave feminism, reflects what Foucault refers to as surveillance, a form of micro social control. It can be argued that this surveillance sustains hetero reality and the heterosexual gender order.

By breaking the causal line between sex, gender and desire, and disturbing the binary systems of sex and gender, the female appropriation of a mannish/butch gender, linked with lesbian desire, can be viewed in two ways. Firstly, as anti feminist, since the adoption of masculinity positions women within the systems of patriarchy, that is masculine women collude with the mechanism of oppression and domination. Secondly as a form of subversion, one which destabilizes dominant notions surrounding heterosexuality, the concomitant construction of the gender order, and the assumption that gender and sex are co-dependent. These readings of the butch continue to be contentious issues within feminist and lesbian politics.

Unsurprisingly, the butch identity also gives rise to tensions for women within sport, in particular the specific culture of football in the UK. Kari Fasting's and Sheila Scraton's (1997) research, through its documentation of the 'experiences and meanings of sport in the lives of women in England, Germany, Norway and Spain" (p. 5) shows that "the English players [football] used appearance and clothes to resist the stereotype of being a lesbian player. Most said that they often dressed up to avoid comment about being 'butch'" (p. 5). This strategy of using appearance and clothes to avoid or assert a gender identity demonstrates the "mimetic relation of gender to sex' as described by Butler (1990). Here, issues surrounding gender appear to be relevant for the English players but not the Norwegian players; "Again we notice the combination not-feminine = masculine = butch which doesn't come up in the Norwegian interviews" (p. 7). It is specifically the cultural arena of women's football in the UK which will now be considered.

Football: tomboys and butches

Both the quantitative and qualitative research indicates that for the women taking part in the research 'tomboy' and 'butch' are terms which are coherent. These two female masculinities give rise to anxiety, tension and at times amusement. The women taking part in the interviews often talk about the differences between being a tomboy and being butch. The most clear difference appears to be age related, although Stevi (aged 33) maintains that she would still -'definitely describe myself as a tomboy'. For the women taking part in the research, the association of a butch identity and/or butch image and football is extremely problematic compared to the associated with tomboyism. The questionnaire findings and interview material indicate that both identities, but more so the butch identity, are allied with sexuality. Thus demonstrating the prevailing discourse of female masculinity.

The quantitative questionnaire material offers a socio-demographic picture of 'women who play football'. One of the few open questions on the questionnaire asks respondents; 'have you ever experienced any difficulties playing a 'traditional' male sport ?'. From the completed questionnaires, a quarter of the respondents did not comment, 22% answered 'no' and 53% expressed difficulties. The expressed difficulties are diverse however, themes have emerged and from a possible 26 themes, nearly 10% of respondents refer to issues surrounding sexuality, in particular the association between female masculinity and lesbian sexuality. For example:

> ...playing a traditional male sport people stereotype and assume
> you are a butch lesbian, which clearly I am not. (no. 268)

> Only the image that is portrayed — although it is improving women
> footballers have stereotypes attached to them e.g. butch, gay and it
> seems to roller coaster tarnishing all players. (no.149)

During the interviews this theme was continued and many of the women
taking part talked about the equation established between football,
masculinity and sexuality. For instance, when the women were asked 'what
stereotypes of women footballers are there?' the butch lesbian identity and
or image was constantly referred to.

> ...There's the obvious one that every one who plays is lesbian, every
> one who plays looks a certain way, has short hair, is very
> masculine, very butch. (Robyn, aged 21)

> I think that every one thinks that erm... just cos you play football
> you're gay... and you are this big butch, you know, hulking around
> sort of thing. (Danny, aged 31)

> Most stereotypes [pause] that they're all lesbians, and that they're
> all butch and we just want to be men. (Sam, aged 24)

Here, the explicit links between lesbian sexuality and butch suggests that
a depletion of femininity is read not only in terms of gender deviance but
also sexual variance. Unlike the reference to tomboy, butch does not appear
in the research findings without being attached to lesbian sexuality. This
strong association functions in two ways. Firstly, in a way Sally Munt
(1998) describes as the "gospel of lesbianism, inevitably interpreted as the
true revelation of female homosexuality... Explicitly and implicitly the butch
stands for the lesbian in the Lesbian Imaginary" (p. 54). This monolithic
image of lesbian experience suggests that masculinity in women represents
authentic lesbian sexuality. Such an explanation fails to take account of
other lesbian genders such as 'femme' and the androgynous style.
Secondly, it functions as a major belief, a prevailing explanation, a myth,
of who plays and why they play.

There has been limited direct research on the butch identity in sport.
Susan Cahn (1996) suggests the "mannish lesbian athlete has acted as a
"powerful but unarticulated 'bogey woman' of sport" (p. 41). This silence is
not evident within cultural studies. In fact Halberstam (1998) theorises
butch to such an extent that she unpacks "butchphobia" (p. 103), explores
butch variability (p. 122) and provides a "glossary of butch" (p. 120). As yet
the butch identity has not been made 'safe' for women in sport. However, as
Cahn (1996) argues the butch is not only a figure of homophobic discourse,
but a real player trying to establish a social and psychic space.

None of the women interviewed professed to being butch and many of them were keen to assert, and tell of how others asserted, a 'non butch' identity. For instance, Chris (aged 32) talks about her experiences playing against other teams — "they want to show everyone that they are not butch dykes, they're girlie feminines who can also play football'. This visual strategy to combat the seemingly ubiquitous butch image can be viewed as a way to "turn the gaze away" (Halberstam, 1998: p. 270) from any signals of potential masculinity. During the research it was clear that the butch identity and image in football gives rise to tensions for women irrespective of their own subjectivity. During an interview with an out lesbian player it was evident that the appropriation of the 'softer' tomboy masculinity was far easier than an affiliation with 'hard' masculine style associated with the butch.

> J: Do you think playing football affects how you feel about your sexuality at all?
> T: Yes it has allowed me to be the sort of person I am which is quite tomboyish.
> J: What are the differences — I mean for you — the differences between butch and tomboy.
> T: I suppose it comes down to... for some reason I always think of someone quite big... someone like... well quite masculine I suppose, very strong. It's like butch I associate it with being ugly and I think tomboy is the sort of nice way of saying that its all those things but they're actually quite cute.

For this player tomboyism is aligned with lesbian sexuality as she demonstrates again here — "I've picked up that there is a view that women who play football are may be quite tomboyish. I know that not everyone who plays football is gay — but there's certainly a sort tomboyish view" (Terry, aged 29). Not all of the women interviewed associated toboyism directly with lesbian sexuality. Most of them consign it to girlhood. Many of the women claim they were tomboys when they were girls, for instance, Jules (aged 43) claims she "was a right tomboy" and Lee (aged 29) describes herself — "I was a working class tomboy". The women footballers in this research share continuities of experience with "top-level European women footballers" (Scraton *et al.*, 1999) who also talk about being tomboys when they were younger.

Although tomboyism has received some scrutiny within sports sociology (for example, see Hall, 1996), there is little evidence of in depth research into women's experience of being a tomboy. Sportswomen's shared experiences of being tomboys as girls warrants further study. In particular, the point at which most appear to dissociate with this female masculinity. Halberstam (1998) argues that "tomboyism for girls is generally tolerated until it threatens to interfere with the onset of adolescent femininity" (p. 268). Sportswomen's reference to having been a tomboy and the later rejection of this form of masculinity poses certain questions. For instance, do sportswomen conform to gender 'logic' through fear of not being read as a woman or is it that sportswomen force themselves uncomfortably into prescribed femininity ? In other words, is it as Butler (1993) suggests a matter of 'abject bodies' or as Halberstam (1998) notes a matter of 'abject genders' ?

Clearly female masculinity exists. For the women in this research the butch identity is understood but avoided, in comparison the women share common experiences of being tomboys as girls. It seems that the problematic butch identity challenges the women's understanding of the aesthetics of womanhood. The butch is understood as 'big', 'hulking' and 'ugly'. These signifiers of butch contrast sharply with what it means 'to look like a woman'. From a Butlerian perspective it is gender which marks the sexed body and this takes place within a matrix of hegemonic hetero-sexuality. Within such a 'power field', the adult appropriation of masculinity by women continues to be pathologised and abhorred. Women must look like women — especially if they are involved in activities which have been established as 'male' i.e. football. If women fail to look like women then they are read as abject. However, as Halberstam (1998) points out "it is remarkably easy in this society not to look like a woman, but one finds the limits of femininity quickly" (p. 28). The "limits of femininity" represent gender borders which are clearly marked and culturally maintained. Men and masculinity, and women and femininity are viewed as synonymous. However, gender transivity challenges this stable notion of gender. By acknowledging that female masculinity exists it may be possible to extend existing theories of gender.

Conclusion

This paper has drawn together gender theory as it appears within sports studies, feminist theory and cultural studies. It focuses on female masculinity and attends to the currency of butch and tomboy within sport's culture, particularly football in the UK. It is evident that the figure of the butch represents a site where anxieties surrounding women's gender and sexuality rest, whereas the tomboy identity is less marked as an anathema. Both butch and tomboy are legible identities for the women taking part in the research. They are understood as gender dysphoria and the butch in particular is read as aberrant sexuality.

To date sport and female masculinity has been largely ignored by sport sociologists. Analysis tends towards a focus on endangered and/or depleted femininity. In this way, theorising relies upon a notion of gender as it constitutes the sex/gender distinction and relations to power. In comparison a post structuralist analysis of gender allows for an extension of existing theories by highlighting the mechanism by which gender is assigned and ascribed. This paper makes a tentative offer to theorise gender in a way which would permit an analysis of female masculinity in sport. It makes use of recent research material and documents themes as they appear within an ongoing research project. In all it attempts to expose the academic tensions which exist around our understanding of gender.

References

Anderson, K. L. (1999) 'Snowboarding. The construction of gender in an emerging sport', *Journal of Sport and Social Issues*, Vol. 23, No. 1: pp. 55–79.

Aoki, D. (1996) 'Sex and muscle: The female body builder meets Lacan', *Body and Society*, Vol. 2, No. 4: pp. 59–74.

Baker, A. and Boyd, T. (eds) (1997) *Out of bounds. Sports, media and the politics of identity*. Indianapolis: Indiana University Press.

Birrell, S and Cole, C. (1994) 'Double fault: Renee Richards and the construction and naturalization of difference', *Sociology of Sport Journal*, Vol. 7: pp. 1–21.

Boyd, T. (1997) '... The day the niggaz took over: Basketball, commodity culture, and black masculinity', in A. Baker and T. Boyd (eds) *Out of bounds. Sports, media and the politics of identity*. Indianapolis: Indiana University Press, pp. 123–142.

Bryson, L. (1987) 'Sport and the maintenance of masculine hegemony', *Women's Studies International Forum*, Vol.10, No.4: pp. 349–360.

Butler, J. (1993) *Bodies that matter*. London: Routledge.

———— (1990) Gender trouble. *Feminism and the subversion of identity*. London: Routledge.

Cahn, S. (1996) 'From the "muscle moll" to the "butch" ball player. Mannishness, lesbianism, and homophobia in U.S. women's sport', in M. Vicinus (ed) *Lesbian subjects. A feminist studies reader*. Indianapolis: Indiana University Press, pp. 41–65.

Fastings, K. and Scraton, S. (1997) 'The myth of masculinisation of the female athlete: The experiences of European sporting women'. Paper presented at the North American Society for the Sociology of Sport Conference. November 5–8, Toronto: Canada.

Feinberg, L. (1993) *Stone butch blues*. New York: Firebrand.

Flintoff. A., Scraton, S. and Bramham, P. (1995) 'Stepping into aerobics', in G. McFee, W. Murphy and G. Whannel (eds) *Leisure cultures: Values, genders, lifestyles* (LSA Publication No. 54) Eastbourne: Leisure Studies Association, pp. 93–104.

Gibson, M. (1997) 'Clitoral corruption. Body metaphors and American doctors' constructions of female homosexuality, 1870—1900', in V. Rosario (ed) *Science and homosexualities*. London: Routledge, pp. 108–132.

Halberstam, J. (1998) *Female masculinity*. London: Duke University Press.

Hall, M. A. (1990) 'How should we theorize gender in the context of sport?', in M. Messner and F. Sabo (eds) *Sport, men, and the gender order: Critical feminist perspectives*. Leeds: Human Kinetics, pp. 223–239.

Hall, R. (1928) *The well of loneliness*. London: Doubleday.

Hargreaves, J. (1997) 'Introducing images and meaning', *Body and Society* Vol. 3, No. 4: pp. 33–49.

Healey, E. (1996) *Lesbian sex wars*. London: Virago.

Holmlund, C. (1997) 'Visible difference and flex appeal: The body, sex, sexuality, and race in the *Pumping Iron* films', in A. Baker and T. Boyd (eds) *Out of bounds. Sports, media and the politics of identity*. Indianapolis: Indiana University Press, pp. 145–160.

Hooks, B. (1990) *Yearning. Race, gender and cultural politics*. Boston: South End Press.

Kuhn, A. (1995) 'Muscles, the female body and cinema: Pumping Iron II', in C. Brackenridge (ed) *Body matters. Leisure images and lifestyles* (LSA Publication No. 47). Eastbourne: Leisure Studies Association, pp. 67–72.

Messner, M. and Sabo, D. (eds) (1990) *Sport, men, and the gender order. Critical feminist perspectives*. Leeds: Human Kinetics.

Miller, N. (1995) *Out of the past. Gay and lesbian history from 1869 to the present*. London: Vintage.

Munt, S. (ed) (1998a) *Butch/femme. Inside lesbian gender*. London: Cassell.

———— (1998b) *Heroic desire. Lesbian identity and cultural space*. London: Cassell.

Nestle, J. (1989) *A restricted country. Documents of desire and resistence*. London: Pandora.

Newton, E (1991) *The mythic mannish lesbian: Radclyffe Hall and the new woman*. London: Penguin.

Parker, A. (1996) 'The construction of masculinity within boys' physical education', *Gender and Education*, Vol. 8, No. 2: pp. 141–157.

Pugh, J. (1995) 'The social perception of female bodybuilders', in C. Brackenridge (ed) *Body matters. Leisure images and lifestyles* (LSA Publication No. 47). Eastbourne: Leisure Studies Association, pp. 79–86.

Roof, J. (1998) '1970s lesbian feminism meets 1990s butch–femme,' in S. Munt (ed) (1998) *Butch/femme. Inside lesbian gender*. London: Cassell, pp. 27–35.

Scraton, S. (1987) 'Boys muscle in where angels fear to tread — Girls' sub-cultures and physical activities', in J. Horne, D. Jary and A. Tomlinson (eds) *Sport, leisure and social relations*. London: Routledge and Kegan Paul.

———— (1992) *Shaping up to womanhood: Gender and girls' physical education*. Buckingham: Open University Press.

Scraton, S., Fastings, K., Pfister, G and Bunuel, A. (1999) 'It's still a man's game? The experience of top-level European women footballers', *International Review for the Sociology of Sport*, Vol. 34, No. 2, pp. 99–111.

Sedgwick, E.K. (1990) *Epistemology of the closet*. London: Penguin.

Spracklen, K. (1995) 'Playing the ball, or the uses of league: Class, masculinity and rugby — a case study of Sudthorpe', in G. McFee, W. Murphy and G. Whannel (eds) *Leisure cultures: Values, genders, lifestyles* (LSA Publication No. 54) Eastbourne: Leisure Studies Association, pp. 105–120.

St Martin, L. and Gavey, N. (1996) 'Women's bodybuilding: Feminist resistance and/or femininity's recuperation ?', *Body and Society*, Vol. 2, No. 4: pp. 45–57.

Whannel, G. (1998) 'Masculinities and media represention's'. Paper presented at the LSA 4th International Conference, "The Big Ghetto: Gender, Sexuality and Leisure, Leeds Metropolitan University, July.

Whelehan, I. (1995) *Modern feminist thought*. Edinburgh: Edinburgh University Press.

Wheaton, B. (1998) 'New lads?: Masculinities and the "new sport" participant'. Paper presented at the LSA 4th International Conference, "The Big Ghetto: Gender, Sexuality and Leisure", Leeds Metropolitan University, 16–20 July, 1998.

Whitson, D. (1990) 'Sport in the social construction of masculinity', in M. Messner and F. Sabo (eds) *Sport, men, and the gender order: Critical feminist perspectives*. Leeds: Human Kinetics, pp. 19–29.

What's in a Name?
That which women call softball,
by the other name — fast pitch —
would still be an exciting
men's game

Lynn Embrey

School of Biomedical and Sports Science,
Edith Cowan University (Australia)

Introduction

> While Australia has inherited or borrowed much of its sporting
> culture, this culture has been transformed to such an extent as to
> have become distinctively Australia. (Cashman, 1995: p. 205).

Softball is one sport which has developed 'distinctively Australian' features
because in Australia it developed as a women's sport. When people refer to
softball it is assumed that it is a women's sport. In the last two decades,
however, softball has attracted increasing numbers of male players. Not
only has it been necessary to add gender prefaces but the men have been
most vocal in arguing to rename the sport 'fast pitch' to remove any
suggestions that the game they play is soft or feminine. The men's voices
have been heard by the predominantly female administrators eager to
accommodate more players be they male or female and to promote softball
as a fast, exciting sport. The administrators are ever conscious of the
opportunities created by the bronze medal performance of the women's
national team at the Atlanta Olympics and their responsibilities as host
nation for the Sydney Olympics.

After a brief outline of the origins of softball in the United States of
America this paper focuses upon softball in Australia from an historical
perspective and traces its transformation from a feminine to heterosexual
sport. In both countries softball has drawn only limited academic interest
(Embrey, 1995). In Australia this is not surprising given its gendering as a
women's sport. But with an estimated 30 million participants in the USA
and claims to be the highest participant sport even celebratory works are
scarce (Dickson, 1994; Babb, 1997; Richardson, 1997). The main academic

111

contributions are those from Fidler (1982), Birrell and Richter (1987) and Emery (1994). Of necessity, but of secondary interest, consideration is also given to the emphasis placed on different versions of the sport, especially fast pitch and slow pitch. Many opportunities exist to explore this sport further to determine more precisely the ways in which it has been adapted to the differing contexts of the 100 member nations of the International Softball Federation.

Origins of softball

Softball was introduced into Australia in the 1940s, fifty years after it was first played by men in Chicago as indoor baseball. Between the first game organised by George Hancock in 1887 and its arrival in Australia, indoor baseball had moved outdoors as 'indoor outdoor' and through a variety of transformations reflected in a diverse array of names including kitten ball, mush ball, diamond ball, sissy ball and even dainty drawers. The name softball was coined in 1926 and formally adopted when the Amateur Softball Association of America (ASA) was formed in 1932 (Dickson, 1994). In 1939, Look magazine deemed softball to be the "girls' national game" because more girls played softball than any other sport, rather than because more girls than boys played softball. During the 1930s and 40s softball was an accepted part of American community life. Leagues sponsored by business and industry flourished from the 1920s as shown by the list of male and female national fast pitch champions (Dickson, 1994: p. 164; Emery, 1994: p. 117). Blatant use of female sex appeal also occurred in the industrial softball leagues from the 1940s through to the 1960s. While doubt has been cast on the actual promotional value of sponsors' products, "women attired in satin shorts and shirts" brought multitudes of spectators to the grounds. "The uniform, impractical as it was for base sliding, certainly stressed the feminine qualities" (Emery, 1994: p. 117). However, the affiliation of "talented female players who demonstrated speed, power, and competitive zeal began to strike its critics as peculiarly masculine" (Cahn, 1994: p. 145). As a result it lost its media appeal and was cast into further disrepute through inferences that many players were lesbians. Public support was rekindled during World War II. Chewing-gum magnate and owner of the Chicago Cubs baseball team, Philip K. Wrigley, established the All-American Girls' Professional Softball League which took the place of baseball in the mid-west while the men were serving overseas. Wrigley reversed the negative image by requiring the players to attend deportment classes and to play in skirts which emphasised their femininity and sex appeal as clearly depicted in the 1992 movie A League of Their Own. The name was changed to All-American Girls' Professional Baseball

League and rules were frequently modified to align it more closely with baseball however, in the postwar era it struggled until its demise in 1954.

Both the industrial leagues and the All-American Girls' Professional Softball League favoured the fast pitch softball. In this version the pitcher and catcher dominate the game to restrict batters to few hits. In contrast, slow pitch, in which the ball travels in an arc between the pitcher and catcher, allows the batters plenty of time to assess the pitch and results in more hits and hence more opportunities for all players to handle the ball. Slow pitch emerged as the dominant version of the game in the 1960s. (Dickson, 1994)

Throughout its evolution in the USA, the governing body, the ASA, has been the domain of male administrators.

Softball in Australia

When softball was introduced in the 1940s, team games such as field hockey, cricket, basketball (both 5-aside and 7-aside which was later renamed netball) and baseball along with individual sports like tennis, golf, swimming and athletics, were already established as women's sports although marginalised by the dominant male sports of cricket and Australian rules football.

Three North American men shared the honours for introducing fast pitch softball to Australia and each had his own motivation. Gordon Young, a Canadian physical educator, was appointed Superintendent of Physical Education in the state of New South Wales (NSW) in 1939 and immediately began indoctrinating teachers in its suitability for primary schools for both boys and girls. The small dimensions of its playing area suited the limited playing space available in inner city schools in Sydney while in rural schools with perhaps 10 to 20 pupils it was a game that they could all play. In 1940 Young also took responsibility for administering the NSW division of the newly formed National Fitness Council and used its meetings to share his enthusiasm for softball with his physical education and "Nat. Fit." colleagues from other states when they gathered for federal meetings. Young's wife, Pat, assumed responsibility for organised community based teams for NSW women in the immediate postwar years.

Bill du Vernet, a sergeant in the US Special Services stationed in Melbourne, Victoria, in 1942 during the early part of the Pacific War, sought out young women to play softball matches against the American nurses stationed at the Fourth General Hospital. He recruited some baseball players from the social club of the post office. This 'silly sort of baseball' (Deason, 1993) immediately captured the hearts and souls of this group of women who, two decades later, hosted the first world championships in

Melbourne in 1965. du Vernet had been hopeful that he might have been able to interest young Australian men but after an initial flurry of interest the men returned to their beloved cricket and baseball.

Mack Gilley was a former American semi-pro baseballer. He was recruited to help women who were keen to re-establish baseball in Brisbane, Queensland, immediately after the war. Gilley considered the women's skills inadequate for baseball and encouraged them to try softball. Such was their enthusiasm that, under Gilley's leadership, an interstate challenge was issued to NSW in 1947 thus laying the foundations for national championships.

Softball grew rapidly but at the expense of cricket and baseball which, in comparison to softball, were considered too masculine, although not in the most feminine of educational institutions, the fee-paying girls' private schools where both are still played. Astutely, the early organisers also chose to play softball at times which did not result in confrontations with men for use of the limited playing areas, or to play in park lands not suitable for cricket. By March 1949 the national body, the Australian Women's Softball Council (AWSC), was inaugurated and with such confidence that it hosted a tour by New Zealand at the same time.

As softball flourished in post-war Australia the 'soft' component of its name attracted media interest. The first feature story in the popular press in The *Australasian Post* in March 1949 placed emphasis upon its feminine attributes:

> In return for their interest and cooperation, girls can play a game which every softball addict insists is the ideal sport for women.
>
> Look at it this way: A complete game of softball lasts 1 1/4 hours. In other words a full game of softball lasts just long enough to test the strength and endurance of the average woman without tiring her completely. The game is fast, giving girls exercise in running. No action in the game tends to develop muscles, although girls say the sport melts down excess poundage. (Hoffenden, 1949: p. 54)

One player, Dot Lumsden, was quoted on her perceived improvement in self-esteem:

> "I'm all for softball as a women's sport. Getting out in the fresh air every Sunday has given me a new interest, and improved my health immensely. I was a little nervous at first playing in front of so many spectators, but after a while I found that playing the game gave me

self-confidence not only in the field, but also in my ordinary life." (Hoffenden, 1949: p.54)

Lumsden's reference to 'so many spectators' is supported by photographic evidence which suggests that crowds were substantial and attendance at the Australian-New Zealand Tests was estimated to be in the thousands. (Today, spectators are more likely to be counted in hundreds.) Among the variety of explanations for the presence of substantial spectators the most plausible were its novelty and accessibility. In the 1940s softball was novel not just as a women's sport but in its playing arrangements especially when compared to cricket which took much longer with no guarantee of a result. Club softball, interstate championships and international tests were played in the cities or in the park lands immediately surrounding the major cities, just a short lunchtime stroll for city workers.

The *Australasian Post* noted its social benefits:

> Another Melbourne secretary, Esther Hone, says: "Softball is the one and only game for women. It induces the team spirit and is physically adaptable for girls. Clubs are always holding socials and weekend gatherings, which help otherwise lonely girls to make friends as well as joining an invigorating sport" (Hoffenden: 1949: p. 54) (Note: Hone was better known in softball as Deason.)

Evidence of change occurred when softball next featured in The *Australasian Post* in 1951. The headline clearly showed the shift of emphasis: Softball is not for "Softies" (Taylor, 1951: p. 36). Thereafter apart from match reports, softball, like most other women's activities did not attract media attention.

The AWSC asserted its femininity and independence from its male founders by amending the constitution in 1950 to declare that "all officers of the Council shall be women". This was not a brave new step but rather compliance with the prevailing conditions in Australia where men's and women's sports had separate governing bodies. The women's associations were required to defer to the men's association for international competition including membership of teams for Commonwealth and Olympic Games and even to hosting international events as happened when the Australian Women's Amateur Athletic Union wanted to invite the great Dutch athlete, Fanny Blankers-Koen, to tour Australia in early 1949. The women organised the tour which was sanctioned by the Australian Amateur Athletic Union who liaised on behalf of the women with their Dutch counterparts and the International Amateur Athletic Federation. The AWSC effectively excluded Young and Gilley from national office and coaching national teams. Their wives took far higher profiles but to what extent they were under the influence of their husbands has not been determined.

Anomalies did persist, however. In the Australia versus The Rest match usually played at the completion of the national championships in the 1950s, the coach of Australia had to be a woman but the coach of The Rest could be either a man or a woman. At State and club level, men continued to coach and manage teams. Coaching female teams does not appear to have been a worry to the men involved. Many were baseballers and their expertise was deliberately sought by women in the fledgling sport of softball. Men's baseball was played in the winter so the men were available to coach although there appears to be some elements of patriarchy with the suggestion that they were 'doing the girls a favour'. Many, if not most, baseballers preferred male company at cricket rather than to be involved with softball. Those involved with softball appeared to be very confident of their masculinity. As with other sports and a trend which continues today, the players often rejected female coaches. Baseball, however, opted in the 1960s to change to the climatically more agreeable summer to be played at the same time as softball and so the influence of the baseball players declined.

So committed and confident were the office bearers of the AWSC that they embarked on an ambitious plan to conduct world championships. During a visit to the USA in 1962 three women — Esther Deason, Marj Dwyer and Merle Short — took on the all male ASA who happened also to be the driving force behind the fledgling International Softball Federation (ISF). Despite the men's best efforts to ignore their presence Esther, Marj and 'Shorty' persisted and, supported by the male coach of a visiting Japanese women's team, finally managed, at a meeting held at 12:30am, to gain approval to conduct the first world championship so long as they took responsibility for everything. Having been in charge of their own destiny for almost two decades it must have seemed a major regression to Esther, Marj and 'Shorty' to have to defer to the American male officials. The championship was held in Melbourne in 1965. The men's world championships were inaugurated one year later in 1966 in Mexico City but without any Australian men.

Despite this achievement, softball like all women's sports in Australia was "confined to the periphery" (Cashman, 1995); the women simply went about their own business. A significant change occurred in 1972 when the word 'women's' was deleted from the renamed national body, the Australian Softball Federation (ASF). Occurring as it did at the time when the second wave of feminism was gathering momentum it would appear that the women were alert to the changing social conditions and legislation enacted to eliminate discrimination and provide equal opportunity in all walks of life

(Embrey, 1995). Sadly, this was not the case. Feminism was not immediately embraced by sportswomen whose time and energy were already consumed by the demands of their sports plus their employment and families. Nor was sport a priority for feminists who focused on central issues like employment, income, education, child care, health services and welfare in the assumed hope that rectifying these would see a flow-on to all spheres of life (Stell, 1994: p. 252). The principle motive for the name change was to align with the international body, the ISF. It did raise the possibility of men's softball. The convergence of women's sport and feminism was still a decade away in Australia. Softball was:

> a women's culture construct ... a constellation of shared values, institutions and networks ... women who were excluded from or subordinated in male dominated cultures established enclaves in which they afforded each other support, solidarity, and sisterhood. (Cott, cited by Parratt, 1994: p. 9)

Rather, the ASF devoted its energies to regaining its international competitiveness having slipped from being the first world champions in 1965 to fourth in the second championship in 1970. An interstate competition for Under 16 year old girls commenced in 1970 followed by one for Under 19s in 1974. To this extent softball mirrored the model of men's sports to develop talented young players capable of joining the national team whose ranks were slowly being depleted as the veterans of 1965 retired. Apparently winning was more important than equal opportunities. Unfortunately the creation of under age national championships did not halt the slide and in 1986 the Australian team fell to its nadir, eighth at the world championship. As the ASF grappled with its declining performances it did embrace a more professional administrative style and appointed its first paid executive officer, a man.

A new challenge was slowly gaining ground. Men now wanted to play softball and to compete in the men's world championships. The situation came to a head in the early 1980s after men from the recently formed Western Australian Men's Softball Association bypassed the ASF and sought to affiliate directly with the ISF. The inquiry was referred back to the women of the ASF because the ISF, like all international governing bodies, only recognised one national governing body in each country. In this instance the national association was controlled by women. The ASF then authorised a survey of men's participation. Interest was sufficiently strong enough for the ASF to give the go ahead for the first men's national championship in 1984, albeit under the supervision of women as tournament director and chief umpire. By 1992 men had equivalent national championships as women, namely Open, Under 19 and Under 16. There has not, however, been a compensatory push by men to assume control of the ASF. Some argue that this is because men still only constitute one third of the registered 60,000 players while others suggest — and not in jest — that the men realise they they can have all the benefits of playing free of the pressures placed on administrators, the majority of whom are still volunteers. Indeed, since the national president has been elected independent of the state hosting the women's national championship, only two women have held the highest office. Esther Deason held it from 1968 to 1981 when the present incumbent, Rosemary Adey, took the reins. The males on the Board of Management tend to represent the female side of the sport rather than men's. The second level of administration, the Council, however, includes the presidents of the state and territory associations, most of whom are male. Rivalry is more intense between national and state rather than between the genders.

Expanding the talent pool did not immediately remedy the ills of the national teams. What was needed was more frequent competition for elite players of both sexes. Under the guidance of yet another Canadian, Bob Harrow, the National Fast Pitch League (NFPL) was formed in 1991. The initial intention was to have comparable teams of male and females with identical team names and rosters but in effect it has become a women's competition and a men's competition with the women having more teams. This is understandable since women still constitute approximately two-thirds of national registrations and women are valued more than the men since only women can progress to the highest pinnacle, the Olympic Games. Fast Pitch was incorporated into the title to distinguish the League from the national championships, to project a more vigorous image of the game and because slow pitch finally became an agenda item for the ASF.

Slow pitch had previously been rejected by the women administrators because it was feared that any such innovations would take players away from the established game and weaken international competitiveness. In other words, the ASF favoured the fast pitch version which is really suited only to aggressive elite players rather than the inclusive slow pitch version which encourages participation. In the United States the growth of alternatives forms of the sport has not been deleterious. The ASA prefers to consider softball as a discipline with multiple forms with fast pitch, slow pitch, and now modified pitch being the dominant versions with tolerance for local derivations such as Over-the-line in San Diego, California, and 16-inch ball in Chicago. Perhaps the American experience with the multiplicity of games and names during its first fifty years has encouraged a more tolerant attitude. With in excess of 30 million participants (Dickson, 1994) and an Olympic gold medal the discipline model has suited the Americans.

With increasing numbers of men and the NFPL, the name 'softball' became another regular agenda item for ASF meetings during the 1990s. An extract of a letter included in the editorial of the ASF publication Line Drive presents the viewpoint of a member of the national Under 19 men's team:

> Softball to the male outsider, should be promoted as the hard, tough, and aggressive sport that it is. Promoting Men's Softball as "SOFT-ball", is somewhat questionable, because Men's Softball is certainly not S-O-F-T! Nowadays, Men's Softball, with 120kph drop balls off 46 feet, double plays in less than three seconds, home runs slammed over 250 feet, and all played on less than two-thirds the size of a baseball diamond — it has no parallel and should be promoted in such a manner. (Gill, 1995: p. 2)

In essence the letter suggested that men's softball was a contradiction in terms but what the letter writer failed to acknowledge was that women accomplished the same feats perhaps in more dangerous conditions with a 40 feet rather than 46 feet pitching distance and pitching speeds just marginally slower at 110 kph. Male players counter attacks on their masculinity by citing statistics drawing favourable comparisons with baseball rather than women's softball. As Messner and Sabo (1990" p. v) note "different types of men may have different stakes in the types of masculinities that sport constructs and celebrates".

The term 'fast pitch' is used with increasing frequency. The most public occurred during the screening in 1998 of softball on national television. The ASF commissioned 13 one-hour episodes comprising the final four matches of the women's national championships held in January and men's held in March and five matches from the NFPL held slightly later. Contrary to popular belief the national broadcaster, the ABC, does not provide 'free' cover rather sports associations must pay. The ASF invested a considerable portion of its limited funds and levied each State association — a de facto levy on players — to raise the estimated $130,000 (Chappell, 1998a, b). Each episode included match highlights — particularly difficult when the women's grand final was a very one-sided 12-0 match with the mercy rule invoked — and educational attention grabbers explaining the rules such as the mercy rule and tie breaker, plus interviews with former and current stars. The commentary was provided by a male appointed by the ASF (and who is the manager of the women's softball program for the Sydney Olympics). He was assisted by the recently retired women's captain who was described as co-host but generally provided special comments and did the interviews. In the lead up to the Sydney Olympics the ASF must foster public support although whether or not lunchtime Saturdays was the ideal screening time is open to debate. The ASF had to accept what the ABC offered to secure immediate coverage with options for 1999 and 2000. The title of the program was Fastpitch Softball but it was advertised in television program guides as simply softball. The ASF is optimistic that its bold gamble will quieten the critics who suggest that it has not capitalised on the bronze medal success in Atlanta. Coincidental with the screening of the first episode was a stinging attack upon the ASF administrators in daily newspapers in Queensland, which is the dominant women's state, and South Australia where the female national president lives (Chappell, 1998a, b). What the critics failed to mention was that the ASF has been in constant search of sponsorship but "it's a girls' sport" and despite over 300,000 school and social players it is still a "marginalised" sport (Cashman, 1995: p. 85). Despite the ASF's best efforts the media — especially the newspapers — is reluctant to acknowledge men's participation and articles about men's softball are even less frequent than women's. By commissioning the television episodes the ASF was able to be gender inclusive.

From a personal perspective watching softball on television produced some "tensions between change and continuity" (Hargreaves, 1994, p.6). Women's and men's softball is 'the same but different'. It is the same in the sense that the same rules regulate both but two differences stood out. First, the women's matches had far more atmosphere. The crowds were bigger conveying a message that this was more important. This was possibly because the national championships were played in Sydney which has the largest registrations and a venue which accommodated several thousand spectators (but it was not the Olympic venue). The men's championship was played at the newest facility in Australia in Canberra. The small local population did not draw very large crowds but did encourage them to get as close as safety permits to the action. However, the presence of spectators immediately behind the safety fence 'cluttered' the screen. To provide clearer vision of the action it may be necessary for matches which are being televised to have plain dark panelling such as that surrounding centre court at Wimbledon or in American baseball stadiums, that is to be more professional rather than 'folksy'.

The second difference was the uniforms. The women wore shorts. New South Wales opted for a lycra body suit under their shorts. The image was of athletic females, certainly good for television but sliding pants showing below the shorts looked rather ugly. The men wore long pants again aligning themselves with baseball. It appeared to confirm Hearn and Parkin's (1995) notion that "Dress and (sexual) appearance are explicit and unspoken ways in which sexuality is visible, even though often by engendering an association in something other than itself" (p. 107). The change of women's uniform is recent and has been argued on climatic conditions with

January being one of the hottest months but March, when the men play, can be equally as hot. The women's uniform is another aspect of the practical versus the image dialectic. In the 1940s women wore shorts and blouses because softball was predominantly a summer sport played on grass. The first Australian team wore all white shorts, blouses, socks and sand shoes probably as a carry over from cricket which several had played at an elite level and wartime rationing. They changed to baseball uniforms following the first tour by New Zealand in 1949. In the 1980s teams began returning to shorts with players arguing that it was more appropriate for the heat (but less appropriate for sun exposure!) and because their international rivals — especially the USA and China — wore shorts. By the 1980s most state uniforms were predominantly white with minimal use of state and national colours. During the negotiation of television cover, the message clearly disseminated to the women's state teams was that they would have to consider more appropriate uniforms, that is, far more use of state colours. The players saw it as the opportunity to change to shorts. Unlike in the USA there are no records in Australian softball of blatant use of sex appeal.

Conclusion

The administration of the ASF has remained firmly with women. Hall (1990) observed that "gender is a socially and historically constructed set of power relations yet it is becoming increasingly difficult to sort out what precisely this means" (p. 223). A little further on Hall cited Connell (1987) "there are two possibilities in the ultimate goal of transforming gender relations: One is the abolition of gender altogether, and the other is its reconstitution on new bases" (p. 226). Softball in Australia is not, however, a "transformed sport" (Oglesby, 1988: p. 140) in which women and men play together. It would seem in Australian softball that men are happy to play on the existing bases and let the women do most of the voluntary — power — work in the office!

In essence, Softball Australia is one of "those organisations which subordinate sexuality to the major occupational task ... [even] where that task is explicitly concerned with the physical expression and/or expression of the body" (Hearn and Parkin, 1995).

Perhaps it is reminiscent of a 1908 version in which the first base runner in each innings could determine which direction his team ran the bases, clockwise or anti clockwise (Dickson, 1994: p. 54). At times softball in Australia seems to be courageously running in the opposite direction as a women's sport attracting male players but at the same time it is clinging to traditional female roles by allowing the men to dictate the name of the game.

Postscript

It is possible that the next round of changes will be generated by women as women's baseball is re-asserting itself apparently at the expense of softball. In the absence of any major research, speculation suggests that women's baseball is benefiting from the hype associated with the televising of men's baseball and for the opportunity for young women to be in a sport that is well recognised as a man's sport. Anecdotal evidence in Western Australia suggests that this is the reason that female softballers are going over to baseball because it is seen a more aggressive, team sport.

References

Babb, Ron (1997) *Etched in gold*. Indianapolis, IN: Masters.

Birrell, S. J. and Richter, D. (1987) 'Is a diamond forever? Feminine transformations of sport', *Women's Studies International Forum*. 10, pp. 395-409.

Cahn, Susan K. (1994) *Coming on strong. Gender and sexuality in twentieth century women's sport*. New York: Free Press.

Cashman, Richard (1995) *Paradise of sport. The rise of organised sport in Australia*. Melbourne: Oxford University Press.

Chappell, Fiona (1998a).'Make or break time for softball', *The Advertiser*, Wednesday 6 May: pp. 11.

Chappell, Fiona (1998b) 'No soft options', *The Courier Mail*, Wednesday 6 May.

Deason, Esther (1993) Interview.

Dickson, Paul (1994) *The Worth book of softball. A celebration of America's true national pastime*. New York, NY: Facts on File.

Embrey, Lynn (1995) *Batter Up! The history of softball in Australia*. Bayswater, Vic: Australian Softball Federation.

Emery, Lynne (1994) 'From Lowell Mills to the Halls of Fame: industrial league sport for women', in D. Margaret Costa and Sharon R. Guthrie (eds) *Women and sport. Interdisciplinary perspectives*. Champaign, IL: Human Kinetics.

Fidler, Merrie A. (1982) 'The establishment of softball as a sport for American women, 1900-1940', in Reet Howell (ed) *Her story in sport. A historical anthology of women in sports*. West Point, NY: Leisure Press. pp. 527-540.

Gill, Nathan (1995) Letter to the Editor, *Line Drive*, 5 (2), 1.

Hall, M. Ann (1990) 'How should we theorize gender in the context of sport?', in Michael A. Messner and Donald F. Sabo (eds) *Sport, men and the gender order. Critical feminist perspectives.* Champaign, IL: Human Kinetics. pp. 223-240.

Hargreaves, Jennifer (1994) *Sporting females. Critical issues in the history and sociology of women's sports.* London, Routledge.

Hearn, J. and Parkin, W. (1995) *'Sex' at 'Work'. The power and paradox of organisation sexuality.* London: Prentice Hall.

Hoffenden, Lee (1949) 'Softball comes to Australia to stay', *The Australasian Post.* March 10: pp. 17, 54.

Messner, Michael A. and Sabo, Donald F. (eds) *Sport, men and the gender order. Critical feminist perspectives.* Champaign, IL: Human Kinetics.

Oglesby, Carole (1988) Women and sport. In Jeffrey H. Goldstein (ed) *Sport, games and play. Social and psychological viewpoints.* (2nd edition) Hillsdale, NJ: Lawrence Erlbaum. pp. 129-146.

Parratt, Catriona M. (1994) 'From the history of women in sport to women's sport history: A research agenda', in D. Margaret Costa and Sharon R. Guthrie (eds) *Women and sport. Interdisciplinary perspectives.* Champaign, IL: Human Kinetics. pp. 5-14.

Richardson, Dot with Don Yaeger (1997) *Living the dream.* New York, NY: Kensington.

Stell, Marion K. (1991) *Half the race. A history of Australian women in sport.* North Ryde, NSW: Angus and Robertson.

Taylor, Percy (1951) 'Softball is not for "Softies"', *The Australasian Post,* October 25: pp. 36.

The Androgynous Athlete: Transforming Gendered Space?

Paula Roberts

University of South Australia, Magill

Introduction

This paper details the life history of Shirley Strickland, who, in three Olympic Games, 1948, 1952, and 1956 won seven medals — three gold, one silver and three bronze — more than any other Australian athlete, before and since. In addition to this outstanding sporting prowess, Strickland excelled in other male-dominated areas, graduating with honours in nuclear physics, and, after a career in science teaching, she became a senior athletics coach and manager, before entering politics.

Research in women's participation in sport suggests the same limiting effects of stereotypes and gender (Coakley, 1987; Czima, Wittig and Schurr, 1988; Eccles and Harold, 1991) which are implicated in other female achievement-related decisions (Eccles, 1987), especially girls' choice of education and career (Almquist and Angrist, 1970, Lemkau, 1983). The influence of family in the development of athletes has been acknowledged (Lewko and Ewing, 1980; Scanlan, Stein and Ravizza, 1989), and in respect of female self-confidence and goal setting (Vealey, 1986, Petruzzello and Corbin, 1988; Duda, 1989). A more encompassing family influence on female sport involvement and achievement appears to be a girl's upbringing in a household without prescribed sex roles (Bem, 1983; Sedney, 1987), which many studies suggest enhances sex-role adaptability (Bem, 1975).

Shirley Strickland escaped this stereotyping. Raised in the wheatfields of Western Australia, her participation in athletics was encouraged by her father, himself an award-winning sprinter, and her mother who was deeply supportive of her daughter's success. With only brothers for companions, Shirley's activities naturally enough were masculine and competitive. Her life history reveals a gender-free upbringing which encouraged the development of a synthesis of traits previously ascribed to one or the other gender, a 'life-freeing' amalgam described as androgynous. This unique upbringing equipped her for survival in the gendered space of Australian sport.

Australian sport: 'where blokes are blokes'

Phillips (1990) summarises the achievement of Australian women at the Olympics. Their successes, he argues, were made even more remarkable when viewed against the backdrop of a society "with an unenviable reputation for sexual bias" (p. 181), where sport is the 'very essence of life itself' to many of its citizens (Horne, 1964: p. 37), and where sport has been described as an instrument for the repression of its women (Summers, 1975).

Incongruously, in view of these discriminatory practices, Australia's push for international sporting glory has depended heavily on its female athletes, who have consistently outperformed their male contemporaries. Phillips quotes statistics which clearly illustrate this contradiction. From 1912, Australia's women Olympians have achieved at a standard out of proportion to their numbers. On average, they have comprised only 18 per cent of the nation's Olympians, yet they have won 40 per cent of the gold medals, and women accounted for 10 of the 13 gold medals in athletics won by Australians since 1948.

A basic problem in female sporting success in a society which undervalues women is the challenge to the female athlete's femininity. Cahn (1993) highlights the dilemma for sportswomen of this cultural contradiction between athletic prowess and femininity, and Haig-Muir (1998), in her analysis of sex discrimination in women's golf, sees little improvement over the past 50 years:

> Despite anti-discrimination and equal opportunity initiatives ... Australia's women golfers remain the objects of chauvinistic displeasure on the course and in the clubhouse, and the butt of sexist humour in golfing literature, jokes and cartoons. (p. 37)

A reason for this chauvinism, Haig-Muir suggests, is that sport both constructs and is constructed by dominant views of masculinity and femininity. It is a key institution where males "learn, develop, practice and perpetuate manly skills and values", which establish it as a critical rite of passage from boyhood to manhood (p. 37). However, sport plays little part in a girl's transition to womanhood, for while 'men have been traditionally socialized into sport, women have been socialized out of sport' (p. 37). But this generalization does not apply to all women. There are exceptions, and one of these exceptions is Shirley Strickland.

Shirley Strickland: a narrative of family and sport

Shirley Strickland, the Australian athlete, in three Olympic Games, 1948, 1952, and 1956, won seven medals — three gold, one silver and three bronze — more than any other Australian, before and since (Andrews, 1996). As well as this outstanding sporting prowess, Shirley excelled in other male-dominated areas. She graduated with honours in nuclear physics, and, as well as science teaching, later became a senior athletics coach and manager, before entering politics. This remarkable collection of successes in male-dominated sporting and professional areas is intriguing, and begs an examination of its antecedents.

Born and raised in the wheatfields of Western Australia to a family short of cash but rich in talent, Shirley was the only daughter of a father, who was himself an award-winning sprinter, who won the 1900 Stawell Gift, Australia's most prestigious sprint race. Shirley's mother, a strong and determined woman, was deeply encouraging of her daughter's ambitions (even if the local bank manager would not approve a loan to assist a girl's higher education — a boy's yes, but not a girl's (Strickland, 1997). On the wheatfields, with three brothers as her main companions, Shirley's activities, naturally enough, were masculine and competitive.

At secondary school, Shirley distinguished herself as both a student and athlete. She shone at hockey, netball and tennis, and in one year won both the junior and senior school athletic championships. She was refused admission to study engineering at the University of Western Australia (there were no female toilets in the faculty building) and enrolled in nuclear physics instead. While studying at the University of Western Australia, she was awarded a double Blue in hockey and athletics. She graduated in 1947 with an honours science degree and began lecturing at Perth Technical College in mathematics and physics, and addressed herself purposefully to an athletic career. After she had won a range of State athletic titles, she received her first serious coaching, narrowed her range of sporting activities to sprinting and hurdling and gained selection in Australia's track and field team for the London Games in 1948, finishing with two bronze medals from the 100m and the 80m hurdles and a silver from the relay. Shirley married Lawrence de la Hunty in 1950 and gave birth to a son in 1953. She won a gold and a bronze medal at the Helsinki Games in 1952 and gold for the 80m hurdles and gold for the relay at Melbourne in 1956, when she was 31 years old.

This small cameo of the multi-faceted talents of Shirley Strickland who excelled in a variety of areas described as non-traditional for women, takes as its antecedent a gender-free upbringing which encouraged the development of a synthesis of traits previously ascribed to one or the other gender, an amalgam sometimes described as androgynous.

Androgyny: a 'life-freeing' amalgam

A significant body of research has examined the constraints which gender stereotypes have placed on female educational, vocational and sporting opportunities. Eccles (1987) and Eccles and Harold (1991) for example, note that, despite affirmative action and education programmes, few women pursue careers in the scientific, mathematical and technical fields, or in sport. Eccles has developed a model of choice which suggests sex differences in choice are related to differential expectations for success, and differential values which result from gender-role socialization.

As a model of choice, this allows a focus on individual differences among women. Eccles and Harold argue that these differences result from the influence of parents and teachers who value traditional gender-role prescriptions of appropriate activities, form different expectations for males and females, and provide different advice regarding children's future options. As a result of these experiences, and without accurate information on occupations, young women in comparison with young men, develop less confidence in their mathematical abilities, less interest in studying mathematics and physical science, and less interest in pursuing careers in mathematics and science-related fields or pursuing sporting activities.

The concept of androgyny preoccupied social scientists in the 1970s and early 1980s, then fell into disfavour, only to be revitalised in the 1990s for its utility in understanding how some females (and males) break free of gender stereotypes, and live richer lives. Bem (1974, 1975, 1983) was foremost in revealing the promise of androgyny as a concept for understanding gender-free individuals, and for raising gender-free children in a gender-laden society. Her 1974 Sex Role Inventory (the BSRI) required subjects to self-report by questionnaire on aspects of their personality that could be classified as feminine, masculine, androgynous (a combination of feminine and masculine) or undifferentiated traits.

A major criticism of the BSRI was its polarisation of so-called feminine and masculine characteristics, and the uncertainty regarding their integration in self-identity. In current research involving open-ended self-descriptions, Vonk and Ashmore (1993) report their androgynous subjects as using situational qualifiers in describing their masculine, feminine, and gender-neutral attributes, indicating that they enact masculine and feminine qualities on different occasions. This suggestion matches the findings in the current study which shows females displaying 'tom-boyish' attitudes at times, yet in other settings wanting to be attractive to the opposite sex.

A comment on tomboyism is relevant here. Burn, O'Neil and Nederend (1996) found that childhood tomboyism was positively related to male instrumental qualities of assertiveness and self-reliance in androgynous females, and noted that tomboyism declined at puberty due to social pressure. However, in sporting environments, tomboyism has been seen as an alienating characteristic of female athletes, with some being accused of being 'developmentally retarded' (Haig-Muir, 1998: p. 3; and Crosset, 1995), and their sexuality being challenged (Lenskyj, 1986: p.57, pp. 66-7).

Women in non-traditional areas: survivors in gendered space

Recent research at the University of South Australia has examined the life histories of a group of female computing executives. In personal interviews, reasons were sought for their choice of information technology as a career, and their success in this non-traditional area for women. There was a surprising commonality in the life experiences of the subjects, which a brief summary under the main themes will illustrate.

Family influences on gender identity and career choice: Role of the mother

Most subjects had mothers who had combined outside employment with traditional roles. Many mothers had had unusual life experiences. One, the wife of a senior officer, was herself a high-ranking officer in the British Army. Another was a wartime member of the Royal Airforce. Several had migrated with their families to Australia at the end of World War II, leaving behind an established career (such as teaching), and, in a new country, turned to manual work (fruit picking or other agricultural labour) to assist the family to re-establish itself.

The subjects' narratives described their mothers with pride, sympathy, amusement and affection, and labelled them as 'strong' and 'independent' women. The mothers were the heads of their households, or occupied a joint leadership role. Most controlled the family's finances.

Role of the father in the family

The fathers in general were described by the subjects as 'non-traditional'. One, whose own mother had died leaving a 'helpless' husband and young family, had deliberately set out to equip himself with house management skills, which he had applied in his own marriage. All except one of the subjects' parents' marriages was still intact.

In every case neither parent had exerted direct influence on the subject's career choice, but both parents had encouraged their daughter to believe she could do 'anything she set her mind to'. Of particular significance was parental support for studies in mathematics and science, in which all the women excelled.

One subject recalled her 'privileged' upbringing as an only child, whose father treated her as a 'hoped-for' son. Her father was her constant companion, extending her socialization to adventurous activities and competitive sport, experiences possibly denied her, had she had a brother.

Family relationships

Most subjects recalled that the girls in the family were dominant. Order of birth appeared to have no significance in their choice of non-traditional career. Only two were first born and most came in the middle of the family order, while three were the youngest in their families. Most of their siblings had 'careers' rather than jobs, but some had not worked, or could not work. One subject expressed her guilt that she was confident and successful, but had failed to help her nervous, depressed brother who had left his employment and had since lacked the confidence to seek work.

Many families had done out-of-the-ordinary things. One family had sailed and raced boats. This family's daughter and her husband took their own small daughters on a sailing boat around the world for five years. One of these girls later became an engineer (and another subject in this survey), while the other is presently serving in the merchant navy.

Most subjects classed their parents as adventurous, while others described their parents as 'willing to take a chance' or 'quick to seize an opportunity'. Only one of the subject's parents' marriage had failed, and her father had spent his working life in a variety of situations, farming, then travelling Australia with his children to find work. He currently had a contract for removing sleepers from abandoned railway tracks in the Australian 'outback'. The daughter described her farm upbringing as a 'jill of all trades', and, amongst other things, driving tractors while quite young. She had moved interstate with her father and changed homes and schools frequently without the stress and sense of disruption that might have been expected.

Self-identity

Nearly all subjects could not remember a distinct 'feminine identity' in their teenage years, nor their being influenced by 'prevailing images of femininity in the media or society'. Many used expressions like 'I wasn't "butch" though', or 'I liked boys', or 'I was conscious of fashion and bought the latest patterns to make my own clothes'. One remembered being cautioned by an aunt about her forthright and independent nature, saying 'You'll have to mend your ways, or no one will want to marry you'. The subject commented with some amusement, 'I didn't change my ways, and I did get married'.

Effects of educational experiences on career choice

All subjects reported an easy interaction with males, with their brothers' friends and with male peers at school and university. All except two were educated in co-educational schools, and none recalled feeling uncomfortable in advanced mathematics and science classes. Several reflected that because they had similar or more ability than the boys in these classes, they had no reason to feel different, nor were they treated differently.

Personal epistemological position regarding technology

The subjects were asked questions designed to gauge their compatibility or otherwise with the cognitive styles of computing, matters which have received attention in feminist critiques of information technology (Jansen, 1989; Wacjman, 1991; and Turkle, 1996). All subjects were bemused that computers might be described as reflecting male styles of thinking. They described their own thinking as logical and therefore compatible with computers.

They did not have well-formed opinions on either the impact of information technology on society, although some noted their defensive stance in social situations when describing their work, and being faced with criticisms linking computers with job losses.

Almost without exception, the subjects had chosen their careers on economic considerations alone. When asked whether their career choice had been influenced by notions of 'service to others' or 'desire to work with people' (factors identified with female career choice by Ormerod, 1971; Head, 1980 and 1985; Smithers and Collings, 1981) the subjects noted that these concerns had not influenced their choice, but had some influence on their current job satisfaction.

Perceptions of work cultures and women in non-traditional careers

Many subjects had long standing careers in information technology ranging from ten to thirty years, and none regarded their work as 'non-traditional'. Most had held jobs of various designations, progressing from programmer to senior systems analyst, and some had moved to management. The three engineers (who were amongst the youngest subjects) used computers as an integral part of their engineering activities, and used sophisticated software for modelling mathematical processes and for design work.

Although most of the subjects commented on their organisations' formal equal opportunity policies, none had experienced the need to invoke these. Notable was the subjects' lack of perception of discrimination against them due to their sex, and none had experienced difficulty in gaining acceptance of their professional capabilities.

Summary of research findings

These narratives provide evidence of socialization in homes without gendered roles and expectations, with strong mothers, who, by choice had moved outside the traditional female role. The subjects' fathers were, at most, nominal 'heads of households' and both parents were encouraging and supportive of their daughters' 'non-traditional' educational and career choices. The female subjects appear to emerge from these upbringings with the confidence to tackle any career. Most came to computing by chance, selecting it for its attractive economic opportunities. All had achieved well in mathematics and science throughout their schooling, and they enjoyed these studies. Most were good at competitive sport, and in sports not traditionally regarded as feminine.

And here the findings of this research study regarding the androgynous upbringings of women who excel in a variety of non-traditional areas find a remarkable fit with Shirley Strickland's life story of achievement; exemplary Olympian, scientist, teacher, sports administrator and politician.

Conclusion

The history of Shirley Strickland and other Australian sportswomen at the Olympics becomes all the more impressive when one considers the obstacles they had to overcome in the prolonged struggle to achieve equality of opportunity in sport.

However, as Phillips (1990) points out, Australia's elite sportswomen of the 1950s and '60s were not dedicated feminists who campaigned to break down the barriers of sexual discrimination. This was far from the case. Most had clearly suffered from discrimination on the basis of sex, but were too pre-occupied with their sporting endeavors to worry about gender bias. Leading Australian swimmer, Dawn Fraser, recalled that, even though she was aware that the men got better trips and 'more leeway in their conduct', discrimination 'just wasn't a concept of the time' (Phillips, 1989).

Phillips (1990) suggests there are a number of reasons why Australia's most successful women Olympians did not challenge the discriminatory culture in which they performed. First, equality of opportunity was not articulated in the 1950s and early 1960s as clearly as today, and these women may not have seen the discrimination for what it was. As feminist historians have pointed out, women then were socialised to a kind of normality which placed them in subordinate roles. They expected to yield when men needed the track for training. They took it as a matter of course when men got superior competition and more trips overseas. Perhaps, as was the case with the computing professionals in the study detailed above, these women had not been sensitized to discrimination in their upbringing, and their androgynous world view did not see difference in the treatment of the sexes.

And like the computer professionals (and their mothers) these Australian sportswomen succeeded because they were 'strong and brave', and, as Dawn Fraser argues, were tougher and more durable than the men. 'I'm not sure', she says, 'but maybe some women began focusing too much on being discriminated against and not enough on training (Phillips, 1989).

Again, like the computer professionals, the sportswomen of Strickland and Fraser's era were in a minority, and they did not threaten male dominance in general nor challenge the masculine values which underpinned these activities.

Women's success on these terms produced a hollow victory, in which women were quickly absorbed into male-centred sporting structures, co-opted by the sporting establishment, and stripped of their chance to bring a different ethic and enrichment to sport (Boutilier and San Giovanni, 1983: p. 18).

A similar concern has been expressed by Roberts (1997) that minority women in the science or computing professions act as 'male clones' because they have absorbed the cognitive styles and values of the masculine disciplines in which they have been educated. These women are unlikely to act as 'change agents' who will challenge the existing norms of these professions. This may be the 'darker side' of androgyny, that it benefits the individual, rather than society as a whole.

And, as Phillips (1990; p. 197) points out, while individual women successfully overcame discrimination to win Olympic glory, Australia itself has never fully capitalised on the potential of women's sport, for male sports administrators, blinded by their own bias, seemed quite incapable of comprehending what women might do for the sporting reputation of Australia if they were afforded equal opportunity.

When the success of the talented women of Shirley Strickland's golden era came into collision with the nation's sexual prejudice, some women won through in spite of the prejudice, but the nation as a whole lost out because of it. The nation's failure to recognise, encourage, develop and sustain the potential of its women for Olympic competition is one of the major missed opportunities in Australian sports history.

Did Shirley Strickland's upbringing in an egalitarian household with a strong and determined mother and supportive father inculcate her with so-called masculine values? A revealing anecdote suggests otherwise. Shirley Strickland, the product of such an upbringing, is courageous, competitive, yet also compassionate. In 1975, a re-examined photograph clearly showed Strickland finishing third, rather than fourth, in the 200 metres in the 1948 Olympic Games, which would have increased her career medal tally. Strickland requested that the matter not be pursued, not wishing the current holder of the bronze, American Audrey Patterson, to be stripped of the medal.

References

Almquist, E. M. and Angrist, S. S. (1970) 'Career salience and atypicality of occupational choice among college women', *Journal of Marriage and the Family*, No. 32: pp. 242–249.

Andrews, M. (1996) *Australians at the Olympics*. Sydney, ABC Books.

Bem, S. (1974) 'The measurement of psychological androgyny', *Journal of Consulting and Clinical Psychology*, Vol. 42: pp. 155–162.

Bem, S. (1975) 'Sex-role adaptability: One consequence of psychological androgyny'. *Journal of Personality and Social Psychology*, Vol. 31: pp. 634–643.

Bem, S. (1983) 'Gender schema theory and its implications for child development: Raising gender-aschematic children in a gender-schematic society', *Signs: Journal of Women in Culture and Society*, Vol. 8, No. 4.

Boutilier, M. A. and San Giovanni, L. S. (1983) *The sporting woman*, Champaign, Illinois: Human Kinetics Publishers.

Burn, S. M., O'Neil, A. K. and Nederend, S. (1996) 'Childhood tomboyism and adult androgyny', *Sex Roles*, Vol. 34, Nos. 5/6.

Coakley, J. J. (1987) 'Children and the sport socialization process', in D. Gould and M. R. Weiss (eds) *Advances in Pediatric Sport Science, Vol. 2: Behavioral Issues*. Champaign, IL: Human Kinetics.

Crosset, T. W. (1995) *Outsiders in the Clubhouse*. New York: Suny Press.

Csizma, K. A., Wittig, A. F. and Schurr, K. T. (1988) 'Sport stereotypes and gender', *Journal of Sport and Exercise Psychology*, Vol. 10: pp. 62–74.

Duda, J. L. (1989) 'Goal perspectives and behavior in sport and exercise settings', in C. Ames and M. Maehr (eds), *Advances in motivation and achievement: Motivation enhancing environments*. Greenwich, CT:JAI Press.

Eccles, J. S. (1987) 'Gender roles and women: Achievement-related decisions', *Psychology of Women Quarterly*, Vol. 11: pp. 135–172.

Eccles, J. S. and Harold, R. D. (1991) 'Gender differences in sport involvement: Applying the Eccles' Expectancy-Value Model', *Journal of Applied Sport Psychology*, Vol. 3: pp. 7–35.

Haig-Muir, M. (1998) 'Qualified success? Gender, sexuality and women's golf', Sporting Traditions: *Journal of the Australian Society for Sports History*, Vol. 14, No. 2: pp. 37–52.

Head, J. (1980) 'A model to link personality characteristics to science', *European Journal of Science Education* Vol. 2: pp. 295–300.

Head, J. (1985) *The personal response to science*. Cambridge: Cambridge University Press.

Horne, D. (1964) *The lucky country*. Ringwood, Vic.: Penguin: pp. 37, 82.

Jansen, S. C. (1989) 'Gender and the Information Society: A Socially Structured Science', *Journal of Communication*, Vol. 39, No. 3 (Summer).

Lemkau, J. P. (1983) 'Women in male-dominated professions: distinguishing personality and background characteristics', *Psychology of Women Quarterly*, Vol. 8, No. 2: pp.144–56.

Lenskyj, H. (1986) *Out of bounds: Women, sport and sexuality*. Toronto: Women's Press.

Lewko, J. H. and Ewing, M. E. (1980) 'Sex differences and parental influence in sport involvement of children', *Journal of Sport Psychology*, Vol. 2: pp. 62–68.

Ormerod, M.B. (1971) 'The social implications factor in attitudes to science', *British Journal of Educational Psychology*, Vol. 41, No. 3: pp. 335–8.

Petruzzello, S. J. and Corbin, C. B. (1988) 'The effects of performance feedback on female self-confidence', *Journal of Sport and Exercise Psychology*, Vol. 10: pp. 174–183.

Phillips, D. (1990) 'Australian women at the Olympics: Achievement and alienation', *Sporting Traditions: Journal of the Australian Society for Sports History*, Vol. 6, No. 2 (May): pp. 181–200.

Phillips, D. (1989) Interview with Dawn Fraser (Sydney, 13 April).

Roberts, P.M. (1997) 'Androgynous women and computing: A perfect match?', in R. Lander and A. Adams (eds) *Women in computing*. Exeter, UK: Intellect.

Scanlan, T. K., Stein, G. L. and Revizza, K. (1989) 'An in-depth study of former elite figure skaters: Sources of enjoyment', *Journal of Sport and Exercise Psychology*, Vol. 11: pp. 65–83.

Sedney, M. A. (1987) 'Development of androgyny: Parental influences', *Psychology of Women Quarterly*, Vol. 11: pp.311–326.

Smithers, A. and Collings, J. (1981) 'Girls studying science in the sixth form', in A. Kelly (ed) *The missing half*. Manchester: Manchester University Press.

Strickland, S. (1997) Television Interview, SBS Channel 28, Australian Television, October.

Summers, A. (1975) *Damned whores and God's police: The colonisation of women in Australia*. Ringwood, Vic: Penguin.

Turkle, S. (1996) *Life on the screen: Identity in the age of the internet*. New York: Simon and Schuster.

Vealey, R. S. (1986) 'Conceptualization of sport-confidence and competitive orientation: Preliminary investigation and instrument development', *Journal of Sport Psychology*, Vol. 8: pp. 221–246.

Vonk, R. and Ashmore, R. D. (1993) 'The multi-faceted self: Androgyny re-assessed by open–ended self-descriptions', *Social Psychology Quarterly*, Vol. 56, No. 4: pp. 278–287.

Wajcman, J. (1991) *Feminism confronts technology*. Sydney, Australia: Allen and Unwin.

Women's Rugby and Subcultural Identity: A Case Study of an Initiation Event

Sarah Taylor
Aylesbury College, Buckinghamshire (UK)

Scott Fleming
Cheltenham and Gloucester College of Higher Education (UK)

Introduction

Rugby union[1] in Britain has a rich tradition that has been described at length in various places (and with variable historical accuracy). In the last two decades however, the role of rugby as a 'male preserve' has been challenged by the emergence of women's rugby as a significant participation sport. Indeed women's rugby enjoyed such a boom in the early 1990s that it was claimed to be among the fastest growing sports in the United Kingdom. Yet in spite of the development in women's rugby (at all levels), the sociological context of women's rugby has not been investigated with the same depth that has characterised some of the subcultural analyses of men's rugby (e.g., Sheard and Dunning, 1973; Dunning and Sheard, 1979; Donnelly and Young, 1985; Schatt, 1996).

Rugby is a cultural form that is constantly being produced and reproduced in conjunction with changing social, historical and political circumstances; and it is a sport form to which different groups attach different sets of meanings, values, beliefs and actions. In order to address the socio-cultural significance (as well as the political and economic impact) of women's rugby, a case study piece of research was undertaken within the context of a higher education institution in a large, culturally diverse city in the UK[2]. The intention of this project was to attempt to ensure that women were placed at the centre of the analysis, and for this, as Jennifer Hargreaves (1994) has recommended, an ethnographic approach was adopted.

This study therefore provides some points of reflection on an interpretation of women's behaviour in a world where rugby remains an area of complexity for the female athlete. Indeed some of the paradoxes are perhaps more evident in a traditionally male-dominated sport than in others. For though rugby can be seen as a transformative and meaningful element in cultural production that may frequently oppose the dominant culture; there is also a sense in which subordinated groups contribute unwittingly to their own domination.

In the sections that follow we consider these paradoxes in more detail. We adopt some of the characteristics of the narrative style (cf. Lyons, 1992; Sugden, 1997) by drawing extensively upon field-notes and interview transcripts, and juxtaposing them with a theorised overview of some of the related material[3]. The main body of the text is structured around two main organising themes: the dominant social order and countercultural challenges. We begin, however, with some brief methodological observations.

Reflections on being an 'insider'

The epistemological and theoretical rationale for the use of the ethnographic approach is well established (see, for example, Hammersley and Atkinson, 1983; Atkinson, 1990; Stanley, 1990), but what is more important for the purpose of this paper is to describe something of the process of doing research, with the assumptions and preconceptions made explicit. We do this by adopting the use of the 'first person' which not only places the 'researcher-as-participant' [i.e., S.T.] at the heart of the discussion, but also conveys something of the life history of the project.

Theoretical analyses of the role of the participant-observer are often characterised by oversimplification. The crude 'observational continuum' (Schutt, 1996) of 'complete participant' to 'complete observer' was much too simplistic for the researcher roles that were adopted during this study. Even the pure types of 'participant-observer role' which accommodate both covert and overt roles as well as active and passive approaches did not go far enough. However the model advanced by Pink Dandelion (1997) does help to clarify matters in the way that the more general context (in this case women's rugby) is distinguished from particular groups (the specific women's rugby club). [The following and later text quoted from fieldnotes is presented in italics.]

Whilst attending another university I had become involved in the women's rugby club and with the subculture attached to it. As a result I became familiar with the broad context of women's rugby (albeit through a single club). I had also played for the team that formed the basis of this study during the 1993/94 season. In that sense I had been an insider to the group; though the reality is, of course, that the turnover of students in institutions of higher education prevents any real continuity of the personnel within teams, and hence subcultural groups are in a constant state of change. So at the outset I was more than merely an insider to the context, but not quite an insider to the group.

At the start of the 1996/97 playing season I embarked on a study of the subculture of a collegiate women's rugby club. I was involved in the club as a regular player throughout the season, and engaged in participant observation as well as undertaking some detailed, in-depth, unstructured interviews with members of the squad. At the same time I was also a post-graduate student, and as such I enjoyed the status of seniority within the squad without being a 'core member' of the subculture.

I did not join the club with the sole intention of doing the research, and initially I went into the women's rugby club as a new member and did not reveal the dual nature of my position as researcher and player. In fact, at the time I thought it was not only inappropriate but also unnecessary to state my position; and I even sought solace and comfort from selectively drawing from a part of an argument outlined by Homan (1991, p. 117): "It may also be argued that public data available in public places are up for grabs and that those who write, speak or behave publicly bargain for the possibility that they will be observed — even by a social researcher".

I was concerned about the possibility of the Hawthorne Effect and how the data collection process might have been contaminated had my role as researcher become widely known. It was not my intention to do covert research, and I was aware of the ethical imperative to seek informed consent — however implicit that might have been. I even had strong suspicions that by 'coming clean' I would not be viewed differently in any way at all. The potential threat to the validity of the data that I hoped to gather presented me with something of a dilemma. Thus in the spirit of 'selective concealment' of the full facts, when quizzed about my research I was prone to glossing over the detail. Only when pressed did I describe the true nature of the work. I became slightly alarmed on one particular occasion when one of the coaches asked some particularly probing questions about the study. I answered openly and fully, and later he remarked in a good-humoured way to some of the players "Did you know Sarah is studying you lot?!". Perhaps the dilemma that I had experienced was merely paranoia because no-one seemed particularly bothered; but it was a real source of anxiety for me whilst I was wrestling with my conscience and experiencing some genuine role conflict (cf. Fleming, 1997).

The specific techniques employed in the collection, interpretation and analysis of the data were of the kind described in detail in a variety of sources (Willis, 1978; Ellen, 1984; Fetterman, 1989; Hobbs and May, 1993). There is, though, a final methodological note which concerns a particular feature of this research with regard to the insider role of the researcher. As Michael Smith (1985) encountered in his study of a public house, the consumption of alcohol can present problems for accurate recall. Indeed when the primary function of a social event is to get those present into a state of intoxication (albeit under the auspices of enhancing group dynamics), the situation becomes particularly acute. As it transpired my status as a post-graduate protected me from some of the indignities suffered by subcultural neophytes, and my low-key demeanour prevented me from being affected such that the collection of data became a physical impossibility.

Situating the subculture

The sporting context within which this subcultural group is situated is a well-established and thriving sports institution. There are numerous connections with National Governing Bodies, the National Coaching Foundation, and other agencies associated with a variety of sports. Formerly an institution for the training of male physical education teachers, it has a history of nearly half a century and has recently expanded a portfolio of sport-related courses. On these courses collectively women students are still outnumbered by men (as are the women on the academic/ teaching staff). There is financial support and specialist coaching available to elite athletes from numerous sports — both team and individual. Importantly too, the men's rugby club occupies a very high profile and receives considerable media attention.

During 1996/97 the women's rugby club had only one team which was drawn from a squad of around 25 players. The team played in the British Universities Sports Association student competition, though it was not involved in a league. The playing standard of the players varied from beginners to regional and fringe international players. It was fundamentally a student driven club, though some aspects of the administration of the club are undertaken by staff of the Athletic Union office. The club was coached by three male coaches, all of whom were also students.

'Initiation' and socialisation

'Initiation' is the term used to describe the first organised social event of the year. Its function was to ensure that alcohol was consumed (to excess) by all the members of the club, and as such it was a deliberate act of identity construction and confirmation, where the existing members demonstrated appropriate behaviours and the new members conformed to the norms and standards set by the hierarchy of the club. In certain ways it replicated a similar set of behaviours practised by the men's rugby club, but the ritualised and habituated conduct of a more embedded subculture was not accepted by these women as unquestioningly as by their male peers. Moreover, in this instance it was a fragile situation and some of the tensions that emerged created a disturbance (even break down) in the dominant social order. We shall return to these later.

Establishing the dominant social order

The evening was predominantly for the initiation of neophytes (i.e., new, first year students) into the subcultural style of the club. All new and existing members were actively encouraged to engage in the event as it was the first opportunity for the new members to prove their appropriateness for and/or adaptability to the subculture. Simultaneously, it illustrated the hierarchical formation of many student sports clubs at this institution, and enabled existing players to assert their own credentials as established members of the subculture.

The initiation event occurred within the first two weeks of term. On the afternoon before the initiation there was a practice match during which all players watching from pitch-side were preoccupied with the initiation, and existing club members retold stories of the legendary antics of previous initiation events which had since passed into student folklore. Inevitably these stories were embellished and exaggerated with the effect that the levels of apprehension amongst the neophytes were heightened. Importantly too, as Donnelly and Young (1988, p. 234) note: "the exaggeration and constant retelling are precisely what make it revealing as a source of subcultural values." However, as if to allay some of the fears, the captain did her best to dispel some of the myths by saying, "Don't worry about it, it is not as bad as the boys, we don't make you drink piss and eat sick". Somewhat incongruously she then added that everyone was told to wear 'number ones'[4] and bring a gumshield.

The back room of a local public house had been booked for the occasion. Activities were organised by existing members of the club

(Captain, Vice Captain, coaches and senior players), and included the implementation of rules, games and forfeits — usually drinking 'fines'[5] — for failure to adhere to the specific rules for the evening. With the consumption of alcohol apparently so central to the subcultural activities, it was unclear how a teetotaller would have been accommodated (if at all) during the social bonding activities of the evening. On arrival for the scheduled start at 7 p.m. everyone was told to get two pints of lager, beer, or cider before they sat in a large circle in the back room. The request for two pints was so that everyone could be required to drink roughly equal amounts, that the drinks would last for a reasonable period of time, and that there was no need to leave the circle in order to refill glasses. The rules and conditions that were to apply during the evening were also made explicit:

Once everyone was in the circle the Chair blew a whistle to get everyone's attention and then explained who was on the committee, and what the rules were:
1. left handed drinking only;
2. no shandy or lemonade allowed in any drink;
3. address the chair in the appropriate manner, i.e.,
    a) hold right breast with left hand,
    b) pat head with right hand,
    c) and say "excuse me chairperson";
4. no looking or speaking out of the circle;
5. everyone drinks when the chairperson drinks;
6. speak only when spoken to;
7. whilst in the circle, no crossing of any limbs.

These rules in conjunction with the initiation event *per se* served (at least) three important functions. First, to assert the ethos of the club through a shared experience of (alcohol induced) ritualised subordination — and even in some instances humiliation. Second, to evaluate the willingness of neophytes to embrace that ethos. And third, to establish the hierarchical social order of the club.

In spite of this elaborate structure for the rules of the games, however, the absence of clear authority from the Captain (the chairperson, and hence a key socialising agent) created some confusion, and ultimately resentment. The neophytes were treated differently from the established players, and the manifest inequity created tension within the overall group. This is a theme to which the discussion will return.

Two countercultural challenges: drinking and singing

During the evening the committee insisted that all of the (male) coaches stood up and 'down a pint' for helping. After they had finished their drinks the coach to the backs (who was also the partner of one of the players) was asked to stand again by the chairperson:

> "Now when you go out with a lad here, you expect him to drink more and be able to drink a pint faster! So as we have a couple here we think it is only fair that Kate [his partner] gets up and you down a pint against each other." At this point both people stood in the middle of the circle and had a race to see who could drink a pint the quicker. Kate won and everyone clapped, both people laughed and then sat down.

This was a clear challenge to the expectations of masculinity associated with drinking. The committee clearly knew who would win the contest, especially as Kate was renowned for drinking quickly. As one of the commended activities within the rugby subculture, it was a 'no-win' situation for the coach — especially as he was likely to have been physically incapable of winning. Had he refused the challenge, his masculinity would have been contested; and in accepting the challenge and losing, he was directly subordinated. The capacity to 'hold one's drink' is a valued commodity that reflects implicit masculine values in certain male dominated subcultures. To be bettered by a woman in this demonstration of perceived masculinity was almost an affront to the coach's masculinity (albeit exacted, perhaps ironically, by his partner).

Later in the evening five of the 'freshers' were called to the middle of the circle for playing well in the practice match. They were each given a Snickers bar with their pint, and they were told to race to see which of them would finish both fastest. Meanwhile the rest of the assembled company sang to them. At the direction of the committee the first song that was sung was *Rugby Men*. This song is a commentary on the inability of rugby men to satisfy their female sexual partners, and also a (very vocal) statement about the perceived marginal status of women's rugby. It also carries some important latent messages about heterosexual values within the subculture.

> *Rugby Men* [to the tune of 'This Old Man']
>
> *Rugby men, they play one, They all take it up the bum*
> *Rugby men, they play two, They can't get it up to screw*
> *Rugby men, they play three, They can't even satisfy me*

Rugby men, they play four, They can't get it up to score
Rugby men, they play five, They all have a low sex drive
Rugby men, they play six, Little boys with little dicks
Rugby men, they play seven, They think masturbation's heaven
Rugby men, they play eight, They all like to masturbate
Rugby men, they play nine, For my vibrator, I do pine
Rugby men, they play ten, Little boys who think they're men
With a nick nack paddy wack, Send the boys away,
[shouted] Women's rugby's here to stay!

The coaches were then challenged to also sing a song. In an almost surreal display of misplaced male chivalry, the men stood up in the middle of the circle and sang their song but only after one of them had given the option of "clean or dirty?" to the remainder of those in attendance. Predictably, the response was "dirty!".

Singing songs in this situation was a deliberate act of identity construction that was reaffirmed by the compilation and distribution of song sheets. For a subculture with a relatively short history (in comparison with its male counterpart), the dissemination of appropriate subcultural activities required the use of strategies that circumvented the protracted period of time often associated with the oral tradition. Interestingly, there was an apparent attempt to include men in the subcultural activities; but this was also an attempt to challenge the imputed masculinity of the male coaches by requiring that they engage in a form of behaviour not normally associated with mixed company. The selection of a 'dirty' song by the women implied the possibility of an embarrassingly subordinated role for the men; for whilst the expectation of a dirty song might imply the objectification and vilification of women and/or homosexuals (cf. Sheard and Dunning, 1973; Schatt, 1996), the female dominated context presented a different social order in which the power relations were at least unusual.

Public humiliation and fractured social order

As the evening progressed some of the tensions within the group began to surface. One of the neophytes was publicly humiliated by the vice chairperson, and this created a hostile confrontation:

Every new player who had played representative rugby was asked to stand, recount their playing background, and undertake a drinking fine. When it was the turn of one particular player, the following dialogue ensued:
Vice chairperson: Who have you played for?
New player: [National] under 18s, development squad, and the senior team

VC: The senior team?
NP: Yes.
VC: Well you'll know Joan Smith then?
NP: Yes.
VC: And Phyllis Parker and Sam Brown?
NP: Yes.
VC: What even Sam Brown?
NP: Yes.
VC: Well you're a fucking liar then because I just made her up!

The new player had clearly been 'set up'. She had made outlandish claims about her playing background which were subsequently investigated and proved to have no accuracy. She was required by the committee to 'down' her pint. This was an example of what Donnelly and Young (1988: p. 228) have called 'the treatment' to which precocious and/or boastful neophytes are often subjected. However the episode did not end there:

The attempt at public humiliation had only been partially successful. The new player did not seem too concerned, she contested the 'fine' that had been imposed, but eventually drank the prescribed amount. The failure to display any remorse at being 'found out' however, was to work against her. Not long afterwards another of the committee members attempted to fine her for "being too cocky". The new player told her to "Fuck off!", to which the committee member got out of her chair and demanded that she drank this new fine that had been imposed. The new player wouldn't, and the committee member became so incandescent with rage that she threw a drink in the player's face.

In the light of this scenario the explanation that the evening was intended to foster group identity and solidarity begins to look rather flimsy. This encounter was not the only demonstration of a neophyte challenging the power of the subcultural hierarchy. As the evening had progressed the drinking circle had ceased to function, and at one particular point the coach said to the captain: "I think you ought to wind it up now, it's been really good girls but I think you ought to wind it up". This paternalism demonstrated by the coach was indicative of the loss of control that had previously been exercised by the committee. A little later the finale to the event occurred:

A girl from the circle stood up and came over to the committee table, took the whistle and went into the middle of the circle. She blew the whistle to get everyone's attention and said: "Right, you lot [pointing at the

*committee] have acted like fucking bitches all night. Now it's your turn
to get up and down your drinks!" To this there was a lot of uproar by the
committee who couldn't believe her audacity to blatantly disregard all
the rules of conformity set out at the beginning of the night. In response
to her suggestions many of the committee stood up and were shouting
things like: "We had to do this when we were in the first year, so you can
do it now! ... No, we're not fucking doing it!". The instigator retaliated:
"C'mon you fucking down your drinks!"*

*With this failure to reassert the social order, and in view of the
apparent misunderstanding of the hierarchical structure of the club, one
of the coaches intervened again and suggested to a couple of the
committee members that the best thing to do was to 'down' their drinks.
This they did, and it appeared to appease the recalcitrant members of
the drinking circle; but with such a manifest loss of control, it was
decided to disband the circle and everyone went to a local night-club.*

VI   Concluding comments

As a sport often associated with the traditionally masculine characteristic
of physicality, as well as the occasional bizarre displays of heterosexual
masculinity, the participation of women in the game of rugby and its
subculture has many potential contradictions. The most significant of these
is the ability or desire at certain times to disregard socially constructed
images of femininity in order to redefine the meanings of actions; whilst at
others to re-establish (and even consolidate) other socially constructed
values of femininity.

This subcultural group disrupted the male heterosexual hegemony of
the rugby subculture (especially in this institution) by playing the same
game, and maintaining the same values of strength and physicality in order
to play it. There were some committed players who got immersed in rugby.
They trained hard, played hard, and enjoyed boisterous socialising with
their team-mates. They drank alcohol, sang bawdy songs, and talked
explicitly about men and sex — often in the company of the male coaches.
There was a willingness to talk openly in front of men about masturbation,
the use of sex aids and sex toys that demonstrated a contestation of certain
societal conventions and norms of femininity.

The analysis of this specific episode in this women's rugby subculture
has highlighted two main issues. First, that the subcultural behaviour
practised by these women shared many similarities with the documented
accounts of male rugby subcultures in other contexts. What is particularly
interesting in this regard therefore is the mechanism through which these

practices are produced and culturally reproduced. (It is important to note here that rugby teams and clubs in general are undoubtedly undergoing radical changes to the social aspects of their subcultural activities — especially at elite levels. The kinds of practices identified, for example by Sheard and Dunning [1973], are not as evident as they once were. There are however two contexts in which such practices may be more evident than others: the student club/team; and the club/team 'on tour').

Second, in spite of the shared aspects of subcultural activity common to men's rugby, there was also an ability to construct their own identity to suit their own needs, and a willingness to challenge some of the societally prescribed notions of femininity. For many, the women's rugby subculture provided a rare opportunity for social transformation — albeit transitory and, for some, fleeting.

This is one women's rugby subculture; and it may be argued that the characteristics identified above are such that this case study is unique, and therefore has no potential for meaningful generalisation. The reality, however, is that women's rugby continues to thrive, and sport-related courses are proliferating at institutions of further and higher education. As with much case study research the rather pithy response to accusations of particularism might reasonably be that this subcultural group will not be vastly different from other subcultural groups like it. And there is likely to be an increasing number of these.

Acknowledgement

We are grateful to Richard Mullen for his constructive comments on an earlier draft of the paper, and to those who contributed to the discussion when the paper was presented at the LSA conference, The Big Ghetto — Gender, Sexuality and Leisure, at Leeds Metropolitan University in 1998.

Notes

[1]   In the interests of brevity, hereafter the term 'rugby' will be used to apply to rugby union. It should not be interpreted as applying to rugby league.

[2]   In order to protect the anonymity of the participants in this research, we have not only adopted pseudonyms throughout, but we have also removed precise and/or detailed descriptors.

[3]   Unless indicated otherwise, all of the indented and non-attributed passages of text are taken from the field-notes compiled during the study.

4 'Number ones' constituted the uniform worn by members of most sports
   clubs at this institution. For women this was typically a white shirt,
   black skirt/trousers, black shoes and college sweater.

5 'Drinking fines' take the form of a prescribed amount of an alcoholic
   drink — usually measured by a number of finger widths when the hand
   is placed horizontally on the side of the glass.

References

Atkinson, P. (1990) *The ethnographic imagination — textual constructions of
    reality*. London: Routledge.

Donnelly, P. and Young, K. M. (1985) 'Reproduction and transformation of
    cultural forms in sport — a contextual analysis of rugby, *International
    Review of the Sociology of Sport*, Vol. 20, No. 1/2: pp. 19–38.

Donnelly, P. and Young, K. (1988) 'The construction and confirmation of
    identity in sport subcultures', *Sociology of Sport Journal*, Vol. 5: pp.
    223–240.

Dunning, E. and Sheard, K. (1979) *Barbarians, gentlemen and players: A
    sociological study of the development of rugby football*. New York: New
    York University Press.

Ellen, R. F. (ed) (1984) *Ethnographic research — a guide to general conduct*.
    London: Academic Press.

Fleming, S. (1997) 'Qualitative research into young people, sport and
    schooling: The ethics of role conflict', in A. Tomlinson and S. Fleming
    (eds) *Ethics, sport and leisure: Crises and critiques*. Aachen: Meyer and
    Meyer Verlag, pp. 137–150.

Fetterman, D. M. (1989) *Ethnography step by step*. London: Sage.

Hammersley, M. and Atkinson, P. (1983) *Ethnography — principles in practice*.
    London: Tavistock.

Hargreaves, J. A. (1994) *Sporting females*. London: Routledge.

Hobbs, D. and May, T. (eds) (1993) *Interpreting the field — accounts of
    ethnography*. Oxford: Clarendon.

Homan, R. (1991) *The ethics of social research*. London: Longman.

Lyons, K. (1992) 'Telling stories from the field? A discussion of an
    ethnographic approach to researching the teaching of physical
    education', in A. C. Sparkes (ed) *Research in physical education and
    sport*. London: Falmer Press, pp. 248–270.

Pink Dandelion, B. (1997) 'Insider dealing: researching your own private
    world', in A. Tomlinson and S. Fleming (eds) *Ethics, sport and leisure:
    Crises and critiques*. Aachen: Meyer and Meyer Verlag, pp. 181–201.

Schatt, S. P. (1996) 'Misogyny on and off the pitch. The gendered world of male rugby players', *Gender and Society*, Vol. 10, No. 5: pp. 550–563.

Schutt, R. K. (1996) *Investigating the social world — the process and practice of research*. London: Sage.

Sheard, K. and Dunning, E. (1973) 'The rugby football club a type of male preserve: Some sociological notes', *International Review of Sport Sociology*, Vol. 5, No. 3: pp. 5–24.

Smith, M. A. (1985) 'A participant observer study of a 'rough' working-class pub', *Leisure Studies*, Vol. 4: pp. 293–306.

Stanley, L. (1990) 'Doing ethnography, writing ethnography: A comment on Hammersley', *Sociology*, Vol. 24, No. 4: pp. 617–627.

Sugden, J. (1997) 'Field workers rush in (where theorists fear to tread): The perils of ethnography', in A. Tomlinson and S. Fleming (eds) *Ethics, sport and leisure: Crises and critiques*. Aachen: Meyer and Meyer Verlag, pp. 223–244.

Willis, P. (1978) *Profane culture*. London: Routledge and Kegan Paul.

Seeing and Being Seen: Body Fashion in Female Recreational Sport

Kari Fasting

Norwegian University of Sport and Physical Education,
Oslo (Norway)

Introduction

Until recently the body had received little attention in sociology or in the sociology of sport. Shilling, for example, wrote in 1993 that 'sociology has adopted a disembodied approach towards its subject matter', and that it historically has been something of an "absent presence" in sociology. Loy, Andrews and Rinehart *et al.* (1993) have suggested that the reason that the sport sociologists had overlooked the body may be because they had been negatively influenced by the non-body bias in sociology in addition to being exposed to "the disembodied discourses of physical education associated with its 'scientization', performance enhancement ethos, and hegemonic image of the body-as-machine" (p. 70). Recently however this has changed, both in sociology in general and in the sociology of sport. The increased interest in the body, and I would also add, in the sporting body, the gendered body, and the sexualized body, seems according to Frank (1991) to be due to the influence from feminism, from Michel Foucault and from 'the contradictory impulses of modernity'.

This interest in the body has taken place, and is taking place, both in academia and in popular culture. Kathy Davis (1997) writes that different explanations have been put forward for what she calls the "recent body craze". For some like, Turner (1984), Featherstone (1983) and O'Neill (1985), the popularity of the body is regarded as a reflection of the culture at large. For others the interest in the body is primarily a theoretical development, and Michel Foucault (1979, 1986) and Arthur Frank (1991) are among those mentioned here. Others again held feminism responsible for putting the body on the intellectual map. Davis shows how empirical studies about the female body have focused on; a) how women experience their bodies; b) how women's bodies are implicated in various social and cultural practices; and c) on symbolic representations of the female body. In summarizing this research she states that feminist approaches to the body attend to three problematic areas. These three problematic areas are difference, domination, and subversion. They are "implicated in the analysis of women's bodily experiences and embodied practices as well as in studies of how the female body is constructed in different cultures, social contexts and historical epochs" (p. 7).

Ann Hall (1996) has focused on the fact that many of the studies of female sporting bodies, particularly in aerobics and bodybuilding, have been analyses of texts or video, and thereby have not taken into account women's subjective experiences. She writes that:

> Cultural analysis based solely on public discourses on texts, without also exploring the meaning of these discursive practices to those who participate in them, provides a one-sided, probably inaccurate picture of the activity or cultural forms. (p. 59)

Markula (1995), one of the few who has explored aerobicizers *subjective* meaning states that the "popular discourse today, at least in North America, invokes a normative ideal of female beauty that is slim, strong, sinuous, athletic, and healthy" (p. 60). 'Athletic' implies that we are now allowed to exercise to build muscles, but at the same time we have to look slim, firm and healthy. In her famous article about the slender body, Bordo (1990), writes that:

> such a perspective helps illuminate an important continuity of meaning between compulsive dieting and bodybuilding in our culture, and reveals why it has been so easy for contemporary images of female attractiveness to oscillate back and forth between a spare 'minimalist' look and a solid muscular, athletic look. (p. 90)

But do we have the same normative ideal in Europe, in Scandinavia? Though we live in very different cultures, we often may be looking at the same TV commercials, and reading some of the same magazines. "Image-making is the cult of modern capitalism", according to Jennifer Hargreaves (1990: p. 20). She writes that the female sporting body has become a focus of consumer culture and been systematically sexualized. What kind of effect does this ideology, combining fitness with sexiness, have on women in sport, on the experiences and meaning of their own and other female bodies?

Methods

The part of the study presented here fits into the Kathy Davis group of feminist studies which tries to understand more of how women experience the female body, both their own and others. As researchers, we were further interested in what this meant for their dieting, their fitness regimes and sport involvement. We wanted, through empirical research in recreational sport, and through the voices of women themselves, to find out what their female body ideal was, how they believed this fitted into society's picture of the ideal female body, and whether each was satisfied with her own body?

The results are from a larger European research project (Fasting *et al.* 1997), which originally was conducted in England (Sheila Scraton), Germany (Gertrud Pfister), Spain (Ana Bunuel) and Norway (Kari Fasting). The main aims of the project were to explore women's individual and social experiences in sport, to find the ways women integrated sport into their lives; and to find what sport and exercise meant for them. This was done through semi-structured qualitative interviews. The following themes structured the interview schedule:

- Sport Biography
- Sport and Social Networks
- Sport and Everyday Life
- Sport and Life Plans
- Sport and Self
- Femininities and Masculinities
- Sport and the Body

The full transcripts of the interviews were analyzed using MAX, computer software designed for qualitative research analysis. The evaluation and the interpretation of the qualitative interviews were carried out according to the principles of qualitative content analysis. This method, allowing a reduction and abstraction of the content of a text, is used according to Altheide (1987: p. 86) "to document and understand the communication of meaning as well as to verify theoretical relationships".

In this paper only the Norwegian data from 21 women active in aerobics (10) and recreational soccer (11) are presented. These women were all members of, and practiced or exercised in, a voluntary sport club. The soccer players were also competing for their club teams in the lowest existing division of their sport.

The participants were between 19 and 36 years of age. The soccer players were youngest with a mean age of 25.6 years while the aerobic exercisers had a mean age of 29.8 years. Most of the women were working outside the home, many of them full-time. Eight of the aerobic exercisers and two of the soccer players were mothers. Traditionally soccer has been a working class sport in Norway. This cannot be traced so clearly in our data, although half of the soccer players had a working class background. Social background was measured by the work of both of the participant's parents. When divided into three categories, almost two thirds of all the participants belonged to the two upper classes.

In relation to education, half of the aerobics women had some higher education compared to 3 of the soccer players. Another interesting background factor was that most of them had started with their sports relatively late in life. Although one soccer player had started to play soccer when she was 6 years old and one in aerobics when she was 7, others had started when they were in their late twenties. The mean age for having started with their sports was therefore 16.1 years (soccer), and 22.7 years (aerobics). The time they used on their sport per week varied from one hour to five hours, and their workouts from 1 to 3 times per week, with an average of 2.1 times for the soccer players, 1.8 for the aerobic exercisers.

Results

In interviewing the participants about their view of the ideal female body, two trends emerged. Some refused to answer the question or to discuss their view of the ideal female body. One said that she had never thought about it, another that she did not have any opinion, and a third one that it cannot be the same for everyone:

> "It varies. It depends on the person; it is not everyone who looks good when they are skinny etc. Some look better when they are muscular." (soccer player).

Others stated that it did not exist or that there should not be any ideal form because "women should look the way they are" (soccer). Women should not strive for a certain norm of what the body should look like. That one is happy with one's own body is the most important thing:

> "I have come to the conclusion that since I always have been a bit overweight, that if one just enjoys or likes one's body, then one shouldn't bother about what kind of body one has." (aerobics)

The other trend was that the female body was expected to be slim, but not too thin, and that it was important to have a female form, at the same time as having firm, and toned muscles:

"One should not look too skinny. That is not nice, but shows that one is a woman, while at the same time looks as if one exercises.... that one cares about the body." (aerobics)

"I think it is pretty to have muscles, but not to be overweight." (soccer)

The message is clear: it is desireable to have muscles, but not be too muscular. At the same time it seems to be important not to be too thin, a feminine figure is also important:

"I think one should have some curves, and be toned, not too much and not too little, as for example gymnasts, with small thin bodies and not like those bodybuilders." (soccer)

These two trends mentioned here, were found for both sports, but there was a tendency that more soccer players focused upon the importance of not being thin but still having female forms.

In talking about society's views of the body, the participants discussed their own opinions, what they believe are other women opinions and the way the female body is presented in advertisements. The trend for both sports is that the female body, as presented through the media, is not identical to the participant's view of an ideal body, and they believe that this holds for many other women and even some men:

"Women are really presented wrongly in the media, because it is not many who have such bodies, and that is what is shown. They should use someone who looks more normal." (aerobics)

"It is often that one believes that those that look like the models are the ideal woman. I don't really believe that. I think that most people like women that are ... that have some shape and who are not so extremely thin, but who have curves." (soccer)

Others mentioned that age might be an important factor. They believed that there is a large relationship between the models and the perception of 15-16 year olds. Some also focus on the fact that they themselves have changed, and that also the picture of the ideal female model body has changed:

"When one was younger then the models meant more. I have many male friends ... it is the girls that look like the models in the media that they turn around and look after in the street, but it is very few

of my friends who look like that. And everyone has one that they
love or who loves them ... I believe that the shape and view of the
body really doesn't occupy us as much as we would like it to."
(soccer)

In discussing if they were pleased with their own bodies, and if they would
like to change it or change some special body parts, both similarities and
differences occurred between the participants from the two sports. Among
the aerobic participants, half of them were not pleased with their own
bodies. They believe that they weighed too much. In addition there was one
woman who was anorexic, who expressed that she varied at lot in her
opinion about her own body. But in spite of this, no one wanted to change
their body through liposuction, or other kinds of surgery:

> "It's the weight yes, that is what it always is about." (aerobics)

> "I believe I have a different view than others have of my own body,
> because I never get negative remarks on how I look. When I talk
> about dieting at work, then they tell me that they don't understand
> what I am bragging about." (aerobics)

The other women who did aerobics said that they were pleased with and
liked their body:

> "I feel that I have been lucky with my body, I have had it with me
> since when I was young. My family never complained about my
> body, and maybe that's why I have self confidence in my body too."

Another theme that occurred is the use of exercise as a tool for changing the
body, or to take care of the body so that it does not degenerate or that one
does not put on weight:

> "If you have not exercised for a while, your arms get flabby. You
> think they start hanging down, and you have to start doing
> exercises for the arms." (aerobics)

Three women said that they think too much about the body, that they are
too preoccupied with the body:

> "When summer approaches you think about the swimsuits and
> bikini and then you just think too much about what you look like."
> (aerobics)

In analyzing the soccer interviews it became clear that they are in general satisfied with their own bodies. No one disliked their body, and two were only dissatisfied at times. "I don't have any problems with my own body, I love my own body" (soccer). Except for one who would not mind fixing her nose, they would not dream of changing their body through surgery: "When you are created like this, you have to live with it in a way" (soccer).

Two of the players think they are too preoccupied with the body, two, too little and the rest think they are unconcerned: "I am of course thinking about my body and appearance, but it is not too exaggerated, though it is not so that you give a damn about it either" (soccer). There is one who talks about the fact that by playing soccer one develops muscles in the wrong places, like the development of the thighs, but no one talked about the meaning of exercise for shaping the body. Some think that they can change their body weight via a change in their eating: "I would have tried the natural method and not have eaten so much unhealthy food" (soccer).

That the soccer players in general are more satisfied with their bodies than the participants in aerobics is also mirrored by the fact that they do not mention the exercise or practice in itself as a reason for losing weight or changing their bodies.

Discussion

The main results of this study can be summarized as follows: some participants refuse to talk about their ideal female body because they believe that such an ideal does not exist, and therefore a discussion about it can be looked upon as meaningless. Most of the exercising women like a female body that is thin, but definitely not too slender, muscular (but not too much); at the same time some mention that to have so-called female forms and curves is also important. According to the participants them-selves, their views are not in accordance with the media presentation of the female body. The media-image of the ideal female body is much more 'skinny' according to our interviewees. Another finding is that many of the participants are relatively pleased with their own bodies. Even if they are not, they do not want to change it through any form of surgery. We further found an interesting difference between the soccer players and the parti-cipants in aerobics. The soccer players seem to be more satisfied with their bodies and may be even more traditional in their view of their ideal female body. What does this mean? Are they mirroring a postmodern society, with contradiction and ambiguity? Are these Norwegian women not so occupied with thinness as seems to be the case in some other countries, and, if this is the case, why? Is it related to the Norwegian egalitarian society and cul-ture in which the naturalness of both sexuality and the body combined with a strict law against sexist advertisements may play a part? As a result, the media-image of the female body may be slightly different than the one found in North American culture, from which much of the writing of the female body occurs. Article 22 in the Norwegian Act on Gender Equality states:

> An advertiser and anyone who creates advertising matter shall ensure that the advertisement does not conflict with the inherent parity between the sexes and that it does not imply any derogatory judgment of either sex or portray a woman or a man in an offensive manner.

I have observed that women in bikinis on the front of a car, for example, seem to sell cars in other countries. In Norway such an advertisement would not have been permitted.

In trying to understand the data, Foucault's notions of power are helpful— both the ways he treats power in his first work (1979), and particularly the more complex understanding of power that he introduced later (1980). His notion of "where there is power, there is resistance" can be applied to our data in the following way: the recreational athletes in this study may have internalized society's preoccupation with slenderness, but perhaps the fact that they do not want to be as thin as the models, and also think it is 'nice' to have feminine curves, may be looked upon as a form of resistance. The same interpretation can be argued in relation to the fact that they refuse any form of surgery in relation to changing their body or a part of it. But these results can also be interpreted in another way. Maybe what we see here is an expression of hegemonic femininity. Though these women want to be thin and muscular (a possible contradiction) they still want to 'look like' women in a traditional way through the presentation of so called female forms and curves. It may therefore be looked upon as a form of compliance rather than resistance? An interesting question is whether women who do not exercise would have the same views. Gilroy (1997) found in interviews with English women participating in aerobics both a desire to change their bodies and to lose weight. But in accordance with our results she also writes that there seems to be a "recognition of the unreal nature of the norms about female body shape and size" (p. 108), at the same time as there seems to be a desire to strive towards these norms. Some of the Norwegian aerobicizers can also be understood using such a perspective. The problem for some of them was their weight rather than their body contours.

A relevant question to ask is whether these recreational women have been empowered through their sport and have thereby become more resistant towards the media-image of the female body. In relation to the discussion put forward by Theberge (1987), Gilroy (1989), Fasting (1998a) and others about the empowering of sport this becomes an interesting debate.

According to Ann Hall (1996), feminist analysis of the exercising body has primarily centered on aerobics. She writes that the theme that appears over and over again is "how to reconcile the public discourse of aerobics with an individual 'aerobicizer's' subjective understanding of her activity and her body" (p. 57). The public discourses emphasize, according to Markula (1993), a fragmented view of self by focusing on improving one's body shape. Markula found however that the aerobicizers' relationships to themselves proved to be contradictory: "fragmented in attempts to conform with the societal body image, but yet integrated in the enjoyment of movement" (p. 98). She further found that aerobics was a source of self-confidence and self-esteem for women, at the same time as they worked hard to attain the ideal body.

In another article (Fasting, 1998b) about the meaning of sport in these women's lives, it was shown that neither shaping the body nor losing weight were mentioned by any of these Norwegian aerobicizers. The view of the Norwegian aerobicizers can therefore be interpreted as a confirmation of Markula's findings when she writes that: "It became obvious in my research that the individual women in exercise classes actively create meanings of their selves, but these meanings continue to be framed and constructed by the dominant forces in society" (p. 98).

Another finding was that the soccer players seem to be more traditional and more satisfied with their bodies than those participating in aerobics. One may question if it is more important for the soccer players to demonstrate 'hegemonic' femininity due to the fact that they play a so-called masculine game? By playing soccer they have already transgressed the traditional gender order. Although this is also changing, since soccer now is the largest female sport in Norway. In another paper (Fasting and Scraton, 1997) we found that elite soccer players both in England and Norway subverted, to a certain degree, a traditional meaning of femininity, at the same time that the Norwegian players demonstrated multiple and changing feminine identities depending on the social situation in which they were.

Seen together these results demonstrate satisfaction, ambiguity and contradiction, which again may be interpreted as an example of the diversity and the difference within gender. Whether this can be looked upon as a threat to and a deconstruction of a traditional understanding of gender is, however, more doubtful?

References

Altheide, D. (1987) 'Ethnographic content analysis', *Qualitative Sociology*, Vol. 10, No. 1: pp. 65–77.

Bordo, S. (1990) 'Reading the slender body' in Jacobus, M., Keller, E.F. and Shuttleworth, S. (eds) *Body/Politics: Women and the discourses of science*. London: Routledge, pp. 83–112.

Davis, K. (1997) *Embodied practices. Feminist perspectives on the body*. London: Sage Publications.

Fasting, K. (1998a) 'The feminine globalization of sports — on men's premises?', Paper presented to the conference "Globalization — On Whose Terms?", Institute of Educational Research, University of Oslo, May 7–9.

—— (1998b) 'The meaning of recreational sport in the lives of Norwegian women', *Women in Sport and Physical Activity Journal*, Vol. 7, No. 1, (Spring): pp. 141–151.

Fasting, K., Pfister, G., Scraton, S. and Bunuel, A. (1997) 'Cross-national research on women and sport: Some theoretical, methodological and practical challenges', *Women in Sport and Physical Activity Journal*, Vol. 6, No. 1 (Spring): pp. 85–107.

Fasting, K. and Scraton, S. (1997) 'The myth of Masculinisation of the Female Athlete: The Experiences of European Sporting Women', Paper presented at the North American society for the Sociology of Sport Conference Border Crossings: Sports, Bodies and the Third Millennium Toronto Colony Hotel, Toronto, Canada, November: pp. 5–8.

Featherstone, M. (1983) 'The body in consumer culture', *Theory, Culture & Society*, Vol. 1, No. 2: pp. 18–33.

Foucault, M. (1979) *Discipline and punish: The birth of the prison*. New York: Vintage Books.

—— (1980) *The history of sexuality* (Vol. 1). New York: Vintage Books.

Frank, A. (1991) 'For a sociology of the body: An analytical review', in M. Featherstone, M. Hepworth and B. Turner (eds) *The body: Social process and cultural theory*. London: Sage.

Gilroy, S. (1989) 'The emBody-ment of power: gender and physical activity', *Leisure Studies* (Special Issue), Vol. 8, No. 2: pp. 163–171, available as LSA Publication No. 32 from LSA Publications, Eastbourne.

—— (1997) 'Working on the body: Links between physical activity and social power', in G. Clarke and B. Humberstone (eds) *Researching women and sport*. London: Macmillan Press Ltd., pp. 96–113.

Hall, A. M. (1996) *Feminism and sporting bodies*. Champaign, Illinois: Human Kinetics.

Hargreaves, J. (1990) 'Looking at images: Representation of the female sporting body', Paper prepared for the Sport Sociology Programme of the International Sociology Association World Congress in Madrid, Spain, July 9–13.

Markula, P. (1995) 'Looking good, feeling good: Strengthening mind and body in aerobics', in L. Lainde (ed) *On the fringes of sport*. St. Augustin, Germany: Academia, pp. 93–99.

O'Neill, J. (1985) *Five bodies*. Ithaca: Cornell University Press.

Shilling, C. (1993) *The body and social theory*. London, Sage.

Theberge, N. (1987) 'Sport and women's empowerment', *Women's Studies International Forum*, Vol. 10, No. 4: pp. 387–393.

Turner, B. S. (1984) *The body and society*. Oxford: Basil Blackwell.

Sporting Females in Egypt: Veiling or Unveiling— an Analysis of the Debate

Linda Balboul

Leeds Metropolitan University (UK)

Introduction

Colonialism has trapped the discourse on women into the discourse on culture (Ahmed, 1992: p. 176). To prove that the 'natives' are in need of Western civilisation, the colonisers took it on their shoulders to impose their superior culture on the colonised areas. Mitchell puts it as capturing the soul after capturing the body (Mitchell, 1988: p. 95). And since women are the bearers of culture, their situation is always targeted and the first step was the veil. Since then, the veil has become 'full of meanings' (Ahmed, 1993: p. 176), any questioning of its validity is interpreted as questioning of the merits of Islam.

Through an analysis of some of the various arguments on the veil, the starting point will be Kasim Amin's 'Tahrir el Mar'a' (Liberation of Woman) and the counter argument of Talat Harb's 'Tarbiet el mar'a wal Hijab' (Educating Women and The Veil). The debate between these two protagonists is a 'prototype' of the debate on the veil throughout the century.

The early debate

Amin (1899) stated that: "to make Muslim society abandon its so called 'backward ways' and follow the Western path to success and civilisation required changing the women". In the course of making his argument, Amin expressed not just a generalised contempt for Muslims but also contempt for specific groups, often in abusive detail. Those for whom Amin reserved his most contempt, ironically, in a work championing their case, were Egyptian women. Amin describes the physical habits and moral qualities of Egyptian women in considerable detail, arguing that they could be recognised and hence their reputation would be at stake if they did any wrong. Amin accuses the veil of being a barrier to women's development and education, arguing that it deprives them from interacting with society and learning how to live.

Amin's argument against seclusion and veiling was simply that girls would forget all they had learned if they were made to veil and observe seclusion after they were educated. Talaat Harb (1905: p. 18) states that his "main purpose of writing ... was to defy Amin's argument against the veil". He starts his argument against unveiling with a compelling statement on the importance of morality, fidelity and modesty. Then he moves on, saying that the Hijab is the best assurance for those wonderful qualities, defying Amin's religious argument with a different interpretation of the same text. At the end, he puts the question: What is better for women, to veil or to be immodest?

Harb uses the holy text as one source for convincing the reader; he uses many other sources such as 'scientific' research done in Europe by German scientists which showed that German women betray their husbands seven times on average, Belgium women six times, and the British women five times ... (Harb, 1905: p. 63). If unveiling is to emulate the West, it potentially would result in the corruption and deficiencies which result from the absence of the veil. Harb uses the same 'social' practical argument used by Amin yet with different anecdotes. Harb laments that the society was much better before the migration of foreigners who introduced of legalised prostitution and called for the unveiling of women (Harb, 1905: p. 97).

In Talaat Harb's introduction of 'Tarbiet el Mar'a wal Hijab' (Educating Women and the Veil), he argues that the West has always hoped to control the East. Khedive Ismail (an Egyptian ruler in the 19th century), seeking to secede from the Ottoman Empire, sought the help of the Europeans to achieve the goal of undermining the integrity of the society, by the introduction of Western customs into Egyptian society. The anecdote he quotes to prove Ismail's attitude was that when he (Ismail) instructed the Sioufia school girls (some of them reaching 16 years old) to go out with their faces unveiled wearing European hats, as a result "most of those girls have become prostitutes" (Harb, 1899: 4). At the end of the introduction he puts it this way:

> We have long accepted the foreigners' idea, taking whatever they say
> for granted, until we have lost our indigenous characteristics; but
> now we know of their hideous goals towards the East. (Harb, 1905:
> p. 6)

The above is an example of what the Egyptian writer Leila Ahmed (1992: p.
166) labels as 'resistance narrative': Harb is resisting the western cultural
penetration; women's position is one of the tools of fighting such an
influence. The same argument is currently valid, late in the century. This
time, Islamists are resisting globalisation and economic dependence rather
than colonisation. Gamal Abdou El Ez, a well-known psychiatrist, argues in
an interview on the Hijab published in *Akher sa'a* (8/12/92) that Muslims
have to prove their identity against the crimes committed against them in
Bosnia. The issue of gender remains trapped in a discourse on culture and
social integrity.

Reference to the Western woman as a paradigm to be followed or
denounced is a major feature of the discourse on women. A package of
moral laxity, pornography, casual sex, materialism, and the disappearance
of the family is usually assembled by the religious voices. The centrality of
women's position in the progress of the nation was highlighted as early as
in Kasim Amin's 'Tahrir el Mar'a'. The same theme was adopted by Harb
and later Islamists: in 1952 at a conference convened by various Islamic
associations, the Muslim Brothers' representatives declared that "a woman
is the standard by which the nation rises or falls" (Hoffman-Lad, 1987: p.
27).

The common features found early in the century are still resilient late
in the century, even the 'resistance narrative' in spite of the absence of
colonialism. Traditional thinking subordinates women to positions of
inferiority, limits their roles to childbearing and housework. It was noted by
Sullivan (1986) that "Egypt's 'open door' policy has affected the lives of
Egyptian women in a number of ways; it created greater demand and better
employment opportunities in the form of relatively well-paying jobs". The
Egyptian constitution does not discriminate between men and women in
terms of either economic or political rights: in fact it prohibits any
discrimination on the basis of gender. Nevertheless, traditional habits that
tend to depress the status of women still exist. Despite the increase of
female education, there is evidence of little change in attitudes to women as
reported in the national report on women (1994). In brief, the majority of
Egyptian women, as a result of a cultural tradition of male dominance, tend
to view their role as centred in home and family, even if they do have a job
and have a relative contribution in the society, they still picture themselves
as inferior to men.

Women and sport in Egypt

The 'westernisation' of Egyptian society took place toward the end of the 18th century with the French invasion in 1795. This was followed by the British take-over in 1885. The British brought with them a number of new ideas including soccer and athletic clubs. Private clubs, which were limited to foreign nationalities such as the British, French and Italians, were soon imitated by the growing middle-class Egyptians. Their education took place in schools patterned after European systems.

The formation of a Ministry of Education in the early 19th century included a department of physical education which was charged with sport and athletics. The inclusion of sport and leisure department in the newly formed Ministry of Social Welfare in 1939 signalled the beginning of sport services in Egypt. Industrialisation, urbanisation and social concerns led the government to increase its allocation for sport services particularly in the provinces which had seen little change since the pharaonic times.

The first institute to prepare female physical education teachers was founded in Cairo in 1937 starting in a girls' secondary school. In 1937 the number of students was nine; in subsequent years it fell to five and then to two and in 1940 it rose again to three students. After 3 years the institute became subject to the authority of the Art Teachers' Training College for Women. Then in 1946 it became independent and carried the name of the Physical Education Institute for Women in Cairo. This Institute formed the first women's basketball team which competed with other local teams and then on an international level.

The promotion of sport in general and of women's sport in particular through educational institutions is even more accentuated at the university level. The overlap between universities and sport organisations is very clear. In Egypt, since 1960-1970, it has become acceptable for girls in large cities to join sport clubs and engage in various sport activities (Badr, 1981: p. 49). Beck and Keddie (1978: p. 8) point out:

> Recently, veiling and seclusion have become much more complex social phenomena. While the wealthier classes educated in Western ways have increasingly abandoned veiling and seclusion, these practices, ironically, have spread among the lower-middle and lower classes.

One of the women who worked closely with Amin was Malak Hifni Nassef, who reflected the feminist tradition prominent among upper-class women. She was the first to design a ten-point plan to improve the status of Egyptian women which she presented to the first Egyptian Congress of

1911. She included in her plan primary and secondary opportunities for females, freedom for any girl or woman to study whatever she liked (cited in Ahmed, 1992). These proposals were considered too revolutionary and threatening to society and were unanimously rejected by the Congress.

For some 150 years, Egypt has been disrupted. Westernisation, socialist ideologies, and secularisation have influenced the modernisation of Egyptian life and thought. Egyptian people are challenged by innovation resulting from westernisation, secularisation, and mass media which have brought sport into the limelight.

The period from 1974 to 1976 was characterised by rapid development in the field of sport in general, and of sport for women in particular (Badr, 1981: p. 49). Anwar el Sadat urged women to make use of their leisure time (al-Ahram, 1974), and he issued decrees that enabled women to participate in the management and leadership of sport clubs (al-Ahram, 1976: August 5, p. 28).

One of the key issues is the fact that Islam discourages the free mixing of the sexes such as happens in the Western world. It would be worthwhile to examine some of the reasons why free mixing of the sexes is so frowned upon by Muslims.

The primary reason why this is not encouraged is that it may lead to illicit relationships. The social problems resulting from such relationships are then documented. The number of illegitimate children are seen to be rising, young girls are seen to be left bringing up young children alone. The biological consequences are also pointed to, particularly the possibility of contracting sexually transmitted diseases.

Muslims see modesty as a protection for them, their health, mental and physical well-being, their chastity and their honour. It is widely assumed that Islam imposes seclusion and dress restrictions only on women, and has nothing to say about men. However, according to Quran and practice of the Prophet, both men and women are required to adhere to certain standards of modesty in their dress and behaviour.

The hijab in schools and universities

In 1994, Dr. Hussein Kamel Bahaa'El-Din, Minister of Education, fuelled the battle on the veil with decree No. 113 preventing school administrations from imposing the hijab on girls. Given the symbolic importance of the veil, the decree mobilised many writers into attacking or defending the Minister's position.

What made things more difficult was a 'fatwa' issued by an Al-Azhar committee denouncing the Minister's decision and considering it an assault on the religious teachings. The thread was picked up by the government's opposition, and papers like *Al-Ahrar* came out with headlines like: 'The Volcano of Anger sweeps Egypt because of the Minister's decree'; 'Parents beg the Minister to have Mercy'; 'The Minister is appealing to the lime lights with his decree ... ' (*Al-Ahrar*, 1994: Sept. 5, p. 94).

The whole issue was turned into a political issue: it was not a matter of wearing the veil or not. The Minister's decree did not say that girls should not wear it, he said rather that parent's approval should be obtained first and that it was not an obligation in order to attend school. Yet, given the political tension between Islamic groups and the government, the decree was considered an aggression on the latter's domain specifically within the administration of the schools which impose the hijab sometimes on girls as young as six years old.

Islam: the culture and religion

Islamic ethic is based upon respect for the body and soul, entailing the improvement of both spiritual and physical aspects of being. The happiness of the human being consists of a harmony between the physical activities which strengthen the body and the intellectual efforts which illuminate the soul (Shaltut, 1966). Prophet Muhammed was an enthusiastic advocate of the health and care of the body, saying:

> ...anyone who has a healthy body is secure, is able to meet his every day tasks and own the world. (quoted in Sfeir, 1985: p. 293)

Muhammed did not differentiate between the sexes and favoured physical activities as a right for both girls and boys as he commanded: 'Haqq al-walad ala al-waled an youallimahou al kitabat wa al-sibahat wa al-rami,' ('The right of the child is one of obliging his father to teach him horse-riding, swimming, and archery') (Shaltut, 1966: p. 171). Muhammed used the Arabic word 'walad' which means child, boy or girl, while 'sabi' means boy and 'bint' means girl. Moreover, Muhammed's favourite wife Aisha reported: "Once Muhammed competed with me in racing and I won. We competed again and he won. Then he said, 'This for that" (Shaltut, 1966: p. 172).

Islam is not opposed to women's participation in physical activities, on the contrary, it favours such activities. However, contemporary Egyptian Muslim women do not participate in sports as often and as much as they could. The explanation might be found in an analysis of elements, both internal and external to Islam, fatalism and mysticism, elements which are in conflict with sport achievement and its values which are derived from Western culture.

Islamic religion in no way tries to depreciate, much less deny sport for women. On the contrary, it attributes great significance and function to physical strength and sport activities. Islam has a constant concern with one's body, cleanliness. purification and force. However, social and cultural changes, due to the interaction of Islamic culture and non-Islamic cultures, have been dominant factors in controlling general access to sport. The cultural heritage is so strong that the Muslim woman prototype still remains, even today. Therefore, participating in sport may be considered contrary to the traditional values.

Conclusion

The purpose of the Hijab is not to further segregate Muslim women and keep them cloistered away from worldly affairs, rather, the purpose is to allow them to participate fully as human beings and not as 'objects'. When they are covered according to Islamic requirements, women feel more honoured and respected and do not feel under pressure to 'look good' and to avoid attracting unwelcome attention. The Hijab is not intended to oppress women or make them appear unaware of what is going on in the world. On the contrary, it is enjoined upon the Muslim woman so that she may be seen to be a Muslim woman.

The debate on the veil is never resolved. It is not merely a debate on putting on a scarf or dressing in a certain way; women's dress code has been trapped in the dilemma of identifying with a whole culture, with political and economic factors playing either in the background or the foreground. The common features found early in the century are still resilient late in the century, in spite of the absence of colonisation.

The debate on the veil has been a good excuse for exercising patriarchy over women. The Minister's decree has challenged the political patriarchy of the Islamic groups that wanted to have a say over girls and young women's dress code. Egyptian women use this on-going debate as a 'screen' to hide their own reasons for not participating in sport (especially on the professional level). I would argue that because they are always expected to do the so-called 'right thing', they prefer to wait until this debate has been resolved, which as I have tried to illustrate in this paper, is likely never going to happen.

LIBRARY, UNIVERSITY COLLEGE CHES....

References

Ahmed, L. (1992) *Women and gender in Islam*. Yale University.

Al-Ahram (1974) 'President Sadat asks women to make use of their spare time in his speech to cooperative and private organizations', Feb. 27: pp. 4.

—— (1976) 'Legislation enabling women to head sport clubs', Aug. 28: pp. 12.

Amin, K. (1899) *Tahrir El-Mara'*. Cairo: The Oriental Library.

Badr, S. (1981) Women and Sport in Egypt. International Congress on Women and Sport, Basel, Switzerland: Karger.

Beck, L. and Keddie, N. (eds) (1978) *Women in the Muslim World*. Cambridge, Mass: Harvard University Press.

Harb, T. (1905) *Tarbiet El-Mara' wal Hijab*, 2nd edition, Cairo: Al-Manar Library.

Hoffman-Lad, V. J. (1987) 'Polemics on the Modesty and Segregation of Women in Contemporary Egypt', *International Journal of Middle East Studies*, 19, pp. 23–50.

Mitchell, Timothy (1988) *Colonising Egypt*. Cambridge, Cambridge University Press.

Sfeir, L. (1985) 'The status of Muslim women in sport: Conflict between cultural tradition and modernization', *International Review for Sociology of Sport*, April 20: pp. 283–304.

Shaltut, M. (1966) *Min Tawjihat El-Islam*. Cairo: Dar-El Ahram.

Sullivan, E. (1986) *Women in Egyptian Public Life*. Cairo: The American University.

About the Contributors

Linda Balboul is a postggraduate research student at Leeds Metropolitan University

Jayne Caudwell lectures in the sociology of physical activity, exercise and sport at Leeds Metropolitan University. She is currently completing her PhD on women who play football. In particular, she is interested in the functioning of gender and sexuality within the context of sport, and draws upon feminist poststructuralist analysis as a way to extend theorising on gender, sexuality and the sexed body.

Gill Clarke lectures in physical education (PE) and biographical studies at the University of Southampton in the Research and Graduate School of Education. Her research interests centre on the lives of lesbian PE students and teachers. Additionally her interests are in sporting auto/biographies. Currently she is researching the experiences of lesbian and gay athletes and the history of the Women's Land Army. She has published widely on lesbian PE teachers and recently co-edited *Researching Women and Sport* (Macmillan). She is also an international hockey umpire, having officiated nearly 150 international matches, including the Barcelona, Atlanta and Sydney Olympic Games.

Lynn Embrey is a Senior Lecturer in the School of Biomedical & Sports Science at Edith Cowan University, Western Australia. She teaches in the sports science and sport management programs. Her research interests lie in sports history especially gender in sports such as softball and netball plus media coverage of the Olympics. She completed two terms as National President of the Australian Council for Health, Physical Education & Recreation and was the inaugural president of the Women's Sports Foundation of Western Australia.

Kari Fasting is professor at the Department of Social Science of the Norwegian University of Sport and Physical Education in Oslo, Norway. She is past president of the International Sociology of Sport Association, and is currently the vice-president of the executive board of Women's Sport International. She has recently been chairing a large European study about the meaning and experience of sport in the lives of women. At the moment her area of research is sexual harassment and abuse in sport.

Lesley Fishwick is a senior lecturer in the Division of Sport and Recreation at the university of Northumbria. She teaches sociology of sport at undergraduate level and research methods at graduate level. Her research interest are in sociology of sport with an emphasis in gendering of organisations; commodification of fitness; identity and the body; and sports ethnography. Her general interests include squash, tennis, football and skiing, although these days, far too much time is relegated to the realm of the occasional recreational participant and armchair enthusiast.

Scott Fleming has been with the School of Sport at Cheltenham and Gloucester College of Higher Education since February 1999. Formerly with the University of Brighton and the University of Wales Institute, Cardiff, he has written in different places and presented to a variety of audiences on racism and ethnicity, methodological matters, and 'Fair Play'. He is the author of *'Home and Away': Sport and South Asian Male Youth* (Avebury, 1995) and the co-editor (with John Horne) of another volume emanating from the Leisure Studies International Conference in 1998, *Masculinities: Leisure Cultures, Identities and Consumption*.

Caroline Fusco is currently in the PhD programme in the Graduate Program of Exercise Sciences at the University of Toronto. Before pursuing graduate studies there, she taught at the University of Manitoba in the Faculty of Physical Education and Recreation Studies for three years after receiving her Master of Science Degree Physical Education there. She received a Certificate in Education and a BA in Sports Studies from the University of Ulster Northern Ireland in 1986, and taught Physical Education in Northern Ireland schools. Her Current research interests encompass Queer, Post-Colonial, Psychoanalytical and Spatial readings of women's bodies and sexuality in sport and physical activity. She represented Ireland in international field hockey from 1980 to 1990 at both junior and senior levels.

Ian Jones is a lecturer in Leisure and Sport Studies in the Department of Tourism and Leisure at the University of Luton. He completed his doctorate in sports fan identification at Luton in 1998, and since then, his research interests have continued to focus upon sports fan identities, the concept of 'serious leisure', and more generally in the field of sport, leisure and social identification. His main teaching areas lie in the sociology of sport and research methods for sport and leisure.

Sandra Kirby is a full professor of Sociology at the University of Winnipeg in Canada. She is a sport scientist and sociologist who is interested in research methods and ethics; discrimination and equality; health and well-being; and sex, gender and sexuality. She is a former Olympian in the sport of rowing and continues to link sport issues, feminism and sociological inquiry in her work. Her most recent publications include *The Dome of Silence: Sexual harassment and abuse in sport* (Kirby, Greaves and Hankivsky, 2000); *Lesbian Struggles for Human Rights* (Kirby, 2000), *Feminist Success Stories* (Blackford, Garceau and Kirby, 1999) and *The Changing Nature of Home Care and its Impact on Women's Vulnerability to Poverty* (Morris *et al.*, 2000).

Lesley Lawrence is a principal lecturer in Leisure and Sport Studies in the Department of Tourism and Leisure at the University of Luton with main teaching areas lying in the sociology of leisure and youth sport. She taught Physical Education before undertaking a doctorate on the professional delivery of leisure in education, focusing upon teachers' perceptions. Current research interests include the interrelated areas of: volunteerism, work and serious leisure. She is co-chair of the organising committee for the 2001 LSA Conference at Luton.

Kirsti Leach is a Sport Studies graduate from the university of Northumbria. Her main research interests focus on the portrayal of women in the media. Since leaving university she has travelled extensively and taught English as a second language in Norway. She has returned to England, completed a PGCE, and is now teaching full-time. She is a fanatical follower of Formula One racing and active participation in netball and skiing.

Paula Roberts teaches multimedia design, social informatics, and computer ethics at the University of South Australia. Her doctoral studies examined a minority of female computing professionals who flourish in this male-dominated profession. Her research extended to a study of female Australian Olympians who also excel in gendered space. The similarity of their upbringings in non-gendered families of these IT and sporting female elites has significance for the participation of women in non-traditional areas, but, in particular, the question of whether these women act as change agents or are merely assimilated into a masculine culture is the focus of her current research.

Sheila Scraton is Professor of Leisure and Feminist Studies at Leeds Metropolitan University. She is joint Director of the Centre for Leisure and Sport Research and teaches on undergraduate and postgraduate pathways in leisure and sport studies. She is the Course Leader of the MA Feminist Studies and co-ordinated the Gender network across the University. Her major research interests include cross-national qualitative work on women and sport in Europe; South Asian women, physical activity and sport; older women and leisure; women, physicality and sport; women, leisure and the city; leisure and feminist theory. She has published extensively in leisure and sport studies and is a member of the Editorial Board of Leisure Studies and on the Advisory Board of Sport, Education and Society.

Sarah Taylor has studied at both undergraduate and post graduate levels at the University of Wales Institute, Cardiff. She is an active sportswoman and her research interests are principally concerned with gender studies and the sociology of sport, and she has undertaken ethnographic work investigating women's sport subcultures in field hockey and rugby union.

Beccy Watson is a senior lecturer in Leisure and Sports Studies and an active researcher in the Centre for Leisure and Sport Research at Leeds Metropolitan University. Her research interests include the leisure lifestyles of young mothers, South Asian women and leisure, changing work-leisure relationships and their impact on women in changing cities, and feminist discourse.

Leisure Studies Association

LSA Publications

LSA

ONLINE

http://leisure-studies-association.info/LSAWEB

Complete information about LSA events and products including contents listings of all LSA Publications:

LSA offers an extensive list of publications on a wide range of leisure studies topics, produced by the Leisure Studies Association since the late 1970s.

Some recently published volumes are detailed on the following pages, and full information may be obtained on newer and forthcoming LSA volumes from:

LSA Publications, c/o M. McFee
email: mcfee@solutions-inc.co.uk
The Chelsea School, University of Brighton
Eastbourne BN20 7SP (UK)

Among other benefits, members of the Leisure Studies Association may purchase LSA Publications at highly preferential rates. Please contact LSA at the above address for information regarding membership of the Association, LSA Conferences, and LSA Newsletters.

VOLUNTEERING IN LEISURE: MARGINAL OR INCLUSIVE?

LSA Publication No. 75. ISBN: 0 906337 86 0 [2001] pp. 158+xi eds. Margaret Graham and Malcolm Foley

Contents

LEISURE CULTURES, CONSUMPTION AND COMMODIFICATION

**LSA Publication No. 74. ISBN: 0 906337 85 2 [2001] pp. 158+xi
ed. John Horne**

Contents

LEISURE AND SOCIAL INCLUSION: NEW CHALLENGES FOR POLICY AND PROVISION

**LSA Publication No. 73. ISBN: 0 906337 84 4 [2001] pp. 204
eds. Gayle McPherson and Malcolm Reid**

Contents

JUST LEISURE: EQUITY, SOCIAL EXCLUSION AND IDENTITY

LSA Publication No 72. ISBN: 0 906337 83 6 [2000] pp. 195+xiv
Edited by Celia Brackenridge, David Howe and Fiona Jordan

Contents

JUST LEISURE: POLICY, ETHICS & PROFESSIONALISM

LSA Publication No 71. ISBN: 0 906337 81 X [2000] pp. 257+xiv
Edited by Celia Brackenridge, David Howe and Fiona Jordan

Contents

WOMEN'S LEISURE EXPERIENCES: AGES, STAGES AND ROLES

LSA Publication No. 70. ISBN 0 906337 80 1 [2001]
Edited by Sharon Clough and Judy White

Contents

GENDER ISSUES IN WORK AND LEISURE

LSA Publication No. 68.ISBN 0 906337 78 X
Edited by Jenny Anderson and Lesley Lawrence [pp. 173]

Contents

MASCULINITIES: LEISURE CULTURES, IDENTITIES AND CONSUMPTION

LSA Publication No. 69. ISBN: 0 906337 77 1 [2000] pp. 163

Edited by John Horne and Scott Fleming

Contents

HER OUTDOORS: RISK, CHALLENGE AND ADVENTURE IN GENDERED OPEN SPACES

LSA Publication No. 66 [1999] ISBN: 0 906337 76 3; pp. 131
Edited by Barbara Humberstone

Contents

POLICY AND PUBLICS

LSA Publication No. 65. ISBN: 0 906337 75 5 [1999] pp. 167

Edited by Peter Bramham and Wilf Murphy

Contents

CONSUMPTION AND PARTICIPATION: LEISURE, CULTURE AND COMMERCE

LSA Publication No. 64. ISBN: 0 906337 74 7 [2000]
Edited by Garry Whannel

Contents

GENDER, SPACE AND IDENTITY: LEISURE, CULTURE AND COMMERCE

LSA Publication No. 63. ISBN: 0 906337 73 9 [1998] pp. 191
Edited by Cara Aitchison and Fiona Jordan

Contents

THE PRODUCTION AND CONSUMPTION OF SPORT CULTURES: LEISURE, CULTURE AND COMMERCE

LSA Publication No. 62. ISBN: 0 906337 72 0 [1998] pp. 178
Edited by Udo Merkel, Gill Lines, Ian McDonald

Contents

LEISURE PLANNING IN TRANSITORY SOCIETIES

LSA Publication No. 58. ISBN: 0 906337 70 4
Edited by Mike Collins; pp 218

Contents

LEISURE, TIME AND SPACE: MEANINGS AND VALUES IN PEOPLE'S LIVES

LSA Publication No. 57. ISBN: 0 906337 68 2 [1998] pp. 198 + IV
Edited by Sheila Scraton

Contents

LEISURE, TOURISM AND ENVIRONMENT (I) SUSTAINABILITY AND ENVIRONMENTAL POLICIES

LSA Publication No. 50 Part I; ISBN 0 906337 64 X
Edited by Malcolm Foley, David McGillivray and Gayle McPherson (1999);

Contents

LEISURE, TOURISM AND ENVIRONMENT (II) PARTICIPATION, PERCEPTIONS AND PREFERENCES

**LSA Publication No. 50 (Part II) ISBN: 0 906337 69 0; pp. 177+xii
Edited by Malcolm Foley, Matt Frew and Gayle McPherson**

Contents

LEISURE: MODERNITY, POSTMODERNITY AND LIFESTYLES

LSA Publications No. 48 (LEISURE IN DIFFERENT WORLDS Volume I)
Edited by Ian Henry (1994); ISBN: 0 906337   52 6, pp. 375+

Contents